JESUS-CENTERED YOUTH MINISTRY

WITH BO BOSHERS, CHAP CLARK, MARK DEVRIES, KATIE EDWARDS, DOUG FIELDS, KURT JOHNSTON, DAVE LIVERMORE, JEANNE MAYO, WALT MUELLER, JUDSON POLING, DUFFY ROBBINS, JOANI SCHULTZ, THOM SCHULTZ, AND GREG STIER

RICK LAWRENCE
Executive Editor of Group Magazine

FOREWORD BY DOUG FIELDS

Group

Group resources actually work!

This Group resource helps you focus on **"The 1 Thing®"**— a life-changing relationship with Jesus Christ. "The 1 Thing" incorporates our **R.E.A.L.** approach to ministry. It reinforces a growing friendship with Jesus, encourages long-term learning, and results in life transformation, because it's:

Relational
Learner-to-learner interaction enhances learning and builds Christian friendships.

Experiential
What learners experience through discussion and action sticks with them up to 9 times longer than what they simply hear or read.

Applicable
The aim of Christian education is to equip learners to be both hearers and doers of God's Word.

Learner-based
Learners understand and retain more when the learning process takes into consideration how they learn best.

JESUS-CENTERED YOUTH MINISTRY
COPYRIGHT © 2007 RICK LAWRENCE

Visit our Web site at **www.group.com**

CREDITS
Editor: Mike Nappa
Chief Creative Officer: Joani Schultz
Copy Editor: Daniel Birks
Art Director: Jeff Storm
Cover Art: Jeff Storm
Interior Designer: The DesignWorks Group
Production Manager: DeAnne Lear

Unless otherwise noted, Scripture taken from the HOLY BIBLE, NEW INTERNATIONAL VERSION®. Copyright © 1973, 1978, 1984 by International Bible Society. Used by permission of Zondervan Publishing House. All rights reserved.

Scripture quotations marked NASB are taken from the NEW AMERICAN STANDARD BIBLE®. Copyright © 1960, 1962, 1963, 1968, 1971, 1972, 1973, 1975, 1977, 1995 by The Lockman Foundation. Used by permission.

The Web site addresses included in this book are offered only as a resource and/or reference for the reader. The inclusion of these Web sites is not intended, in any way, to be interpreted as an endorsement of these sites or their content on the part of Group Publishing, Inc., or the author. In addition, the author and Group Publishing, Inc., do not vouch for the content of these Web sites for the life of this book.

LIBRARY OF CONGRESS CATALOGING-IN-PUBLICATION DATA

Lawrence, Rick, 1961-
 Jesus-centered youth ministry / Rick Lawrence.
   p. cm.
 ISBN 978-0-7644-3504-1 (pbk. : alk. paper)
 1. Church work with youth. 2. Jesus Christ--Person and offices--Study and teaching. I. Title.
 BV4447.L38 2007
 259'.23--dc22
                              2006101607

ISBN 978-0-7644-3504-1

10 9 8 7 6 5 4 3 2 1 09 08 07

DEDICATION

For my two girls, Lucy and Emma,
in honor of the beeline you're already following.
—RL

●

ACKNOWLEDGMENTS

- For the "blacksmiths" in my life who've partnered with God to shape me into a desperate-for-Jesus sort of man: Most importantly, my wife Bev—your love for my heart has carried it to Jesus. And for Bob Krulish, Tom Melton, Ned Erickson, Dave and Georgia Rhodes, Doug Ashley, and Brad Behan—people who are still swinging their smithy's hammer in my life. And for the hall-of-fame blacksmiths: Scot Douglas and Bill Rader.

- For the "wordsmiths" in my life who've made this book better, just because they could: Mike Nappa, my editor, and the hodgepodge of people who read the manuscript and gave me valued feedback.

- For my parents, who pointed me "in the way I should go" toward Jesus when I was young and know now that "I've not departed from it."

- For Thom and Joani Schultz, who have mentored me in so many ways.

- For the musicians who prodded me as I worked: Van Morrison, Counting Crows, The Normals, Andrew Osenga, Andrew Peterson, Michael Card, Jars of Clay, Bob Dylan, Ben Harper, Elvis Costello, Patty Griffin, Lucinda Williams, Frank Sinatra, and U2, among many others.

CONTENTS

Foreword by Doug Fields 9

Introduction 11

PART ONE: THE BEELINE IMPERATIVE

One: The Spurgeon Way 19

Two: This Changes Everything 25

Three: Do We Know What We Think We Know? 34

Four: Deconstructing the Trojan Horse 45

PART TWO: JESUS-CENTERED YOUTH MINISTRY

Five: Discipleship (With an Introduction by Duffy Robbins).................... 61

Six: Mentoring (With an Introduction by Bo Boshers and
     Judson Poling) 84

Seven: Evangelism (With an Introduction by Greg Stier) 95

Eight: Small Groups (With an Introduction by Jeanne Mayo) 103

Nine: Outreach (With an Introduction by Dave Livermore) 111

Ten: Engaging Culture (With an Introduction by Walt Mueller) 118

Eleven: Counseling (With an Introduction by Chap Clark) 125

Twelve: Volunteers (With an Introduction by Kurt Johnston and Katie
     Edwards) 135

Thirteen: Parents (With an Introduction by Mark DeVries) 144

Fourteen: Communication (With an Introduction by Thom
     and Joani Schultz) 153

PART THREE: CLOSING IMPERATIVES

Fifteen: Determined to Know Nothing 163

FOREWORD

If you're a youth worker, you know Brett Cervoni. Brett is a youth ministry leader who prepares his messages, assembles the program, and tries his best to organize adult leaders. He's active and busy doing ministry. When Wednesday night rolls around, you can find him setting up the chairs, preparing the media presentation, searching frantically for a funny and/or gross game, and making sure the music leaders don't stink when it comes time to sing. Brett is actively trying to create an attractive and engaging youth ministry!

After all his hard work, the teenagers leave to go home. Then Brett leaves to go home—he's tired, wondering if the program made any difference. He's trying to remember the names of that night's visiting students. He's feeling a little lonely...and a lot hungry. So on his way home he stops by Taco Bell for a late-night binge and runs into a former youth group student. Lindsey was one of the very active teenagers in Brett's ministry—in his words, she was "a star!" Chances are, you know a Lindsey in your group.

As they catch up on all their news, Brett feels a fond affection for Lindsey. He tells her how proud he is of her, in a spiritual sense, because she seems to be making good decisions about her life and faith while she's away at college. Brett is thrilled that at least one of his graduates is walking closely with Jesus. Then he casually brings up the names of a few of Lindsey's old cronies in the youth group—she pauses and acts almost embarrassed about them. She knows they're making some poor choices and living in a way that doesn't reflect well on a follower of Jesus. Her look and the stories that accompany it make Brett sink a little lower. He was happy to see Lindsey but sad when he thought about the kids who graduated from his ministry and were now wandering away from Jesus.

Brett's drive home from Taco Bell seemed long because the questions came fast and furious. What was missing in his teaching? Why did it seem like Lindsey was in the minority? Was he a bad youth worker? Were his programs weak and lacking creativity? Was his youth ministry really working? These were not neutral questions...and it didn't take long for the guilt to set in. Too tired to wait for answers, he fell asleep watching TV.

Do you know someone like Brett? I know him too well. Brett Cervoni could easily be Doug Fields. In fact, he probably is. As I read the book you're holding, I knew what Brett—and you and I—need. I also knew it wasn't going to be easy. I read Rick's work and I was filled with challenge, anger, hope, and confusion. I know Jesus is central. I've been teaching that for years—for goodness' sake, it's Chapter 1 in my book, *Purpose-Driven Youth Ministry*. But I had to ask myself, "Is Jesus *really* central? Is he central in everything I do, plan, create, and think about?" (The answer to this is where the anger—self-anger—may have come from.)

Rick Lawrence has done in this book what he has been doing as editor of Group Magazine for almost 20 years—he makes you think, he loves you, he wants you to win, and he provides you with practical ideas in a journey toward hope. Honestly, I also think he writes some material from an editor's perspective and not a practicing youth worker's. A couple of times I've yelled at him, "Come on, Rick—that's not going to happen in youth ministry—at least not at my church!" But it was also during those times that I thought: "Maybe he's right. Maybe I need to change the way I'm thinking and doing things...maybe it will work."

If you want to agree with everything that's written and are looking for an easy 1-2-3 plan for spiritual health and growth, this isn't the book. But if you want to read and be challenged to think and rethink the *how, why,* and *because* of youth ministry... this will be a great read for you.

Rick wants to lead us to Jesus and force us to think about how our youth ministry and teenagers and leaders would be different if Jesus were central...no, more than central...if Jesus were everything. He's convincing and convicting that teenagers, youth ministries, leaders, parents—and you and I—need more of Jesus and less of ministry. He's got the research, the stories, and the ideas to show youth workers like you, me, and Brett Cervoni how we might change youth ministry by making Jesus central—where he belongs.

I am excited for the impact this book will have on your personal life and ministry. It will energize and encourage you in your call to continue to make a difference in the lives of teenagers. What a wild journey!

Blessings,

—Doug Fields
Youth Pastor, Saddleback Church
Founder, Simply Youth Ministry

INTRODUCTION

ere's mud in your eye!

Six months ago Greg Stier, founder and president of Dare 2 Share Ministries, said something to me that finally cured my blindness. We were sitting across from each other toward the end of a youth ministry brainstorming session held in the Loveland, Colorado, offices of Group Magazine, the youth ministry resource I've edited for the last two decades. I don't even remember what we were talking about, but I'll never forget the casual way Greg metaphorically "spit in the dirt" and then smeared the mud on my eyes:

"Well, you know," he said, "Spurgeon said that no matter what Bible text he was preaching on or what issue he was teaching about, he always made a beeline to the cross, to Jesus."

A beeline to Jesus?

I was blinded by that light. I knew next to nothing about Spurgeon—Charles Haddon Spurgeon, the great British preacher and teacher—but I knew his "beeline to Jesus" had suddenly clarified everything for me. Five years of dissonance and restless exploration now made sense to me in the burning light of the beeline.

●

ack at the beginning of this five-year season in my life, during the heyday of the "What Would Jesus Do?" fad, I started to doubt the foundations of the movement. The central question of the book (Charles Sheldon's *In His Steps*[1]), which the WWJD frenzy was based on, is simple, really: "If Christians are supposed to be following Jesus, why aren't they making more of an impact in their daily lives?" The book's answer was to imagine what everyday life might be like if all of us simply talked and acted more like Jesus. Well, that *would* change everything. But as far as I could tell from my perch as editor of Group Magazine, the WWJD movement *hadn't* changed everything.

Maybe, I pondered, the Christ-following lives we think we're living are actually disconnected from the real Jesus of the prophets and the gospels and the epistles. It's fine to work up my imagined Jesus-response when someone cuts me off on the freeway, but really the whole thing desperately depends on my own intimacy with Christ. I realized something profound: I could miss Jesus entirely by arrogantly assuming my imagined responses to a partially understood Jesus meant I was really following...Jesus.

1 Charles Sheldon, *In His Steps* (Uhrichsville, OH: Barbour Publishing, 2005).

"What does 'follow Jesus' mean anyway?" I asked myself. Have I really soaked in the personality of Jesus—pursued him as the most fascinating, enigmatic, lightning-bolt person who ever lived? I decided to try an experiment. I'd quickly read through Matthew's gospel looking only for patterns in what Jesus said and did. My experiment yielded 15 observations. Here's a summary of what I wrote on my computer as I sat there with my Bible open:

1. Jesus spent more time praying than speaking. Why? I think it was because he knew he was in a fight with a formidable foe who was serious about "killing, stealing from, and destroying" the children of God. When he sent his disciples out on their own for the first time, he explicitly told them to "drive out demons."

2. Jesus enjoyed spending time with self-confessed sinners. Why? I think it was because they weren't shrink-wrapping themselves in man-made righteousness.

3. Jesus said we'd know we were starting to make an impact when people started insulting, persecuting, and defaming us because of him. Hmm.

4. Jesus hated it when people hid themselves behind religious rule keeping, and he told his followers to plunge themselves into the mainstream culture like a lamp in a dark room or salt added to a recipe.

5. Jesus spoke openly about hell and warned there are real consequences for those who cling to self-sufficiency and unbelief.

6. Jesus hated it when people prayed or served or sacrificed to boost their profiles or feed their egos. He honored secret acts because they revealed a desire for an honest relationship with God.

7. Jesus was quick to forgive those who were repentant and quick to condemn those who weren't.

8. Jesus said the richest people were those who'd banked a lifetime of actions that honored God. He bluntly told his followers they could *not* be motivated by love of money and love of God at the same time.

9. Jesus told us to ignore people who talk big but don't act big and to honor those who talk small but act big.

10. Jesus healed people of incurable diseases and permanent disabilities.

11. Jesus loved celebrations and enjoyed himself so much that the religious rule keepers accused him of public drunkenness.

12. Jesus said, metaphorically, that farmers who sat around in the farmhouse waiting for corncobs to launch themselves through the door were sadly misinformed about the concept of "harvesting."

13. Jesus said our loyalty to him and his ways should outweigh our loyalty to our biological family and its traditions and practices.

14. Jesus told us not to focus our energies on fighting sin (pulling weeds), but instead to do everything we can to encourage good growth (growing wheat).
15. Finally, Jesus said the root of our lack of faith is our penchant to forget the acts and character of God—our biggest faith battle is remembering to remember God.

When I finished my experiment and sat back to soak in what I'd written, I was startled by how Jesus was so consistently offensive to my American Christian sensibilities, "inalienable rights," and everyday self-absorbed behaviors.

And I was also passionately drawn to him.

In Mark Galli's excellent book *Jesus Mean and Wild*, he describes a similar startling encounter with an unmasked Jesus. Galli was pastor of a California church when a group of Laotian refugees asked if they could become members. Galli offered to lead them through a study of Mark's gospel as a foundational exercise before they made their commitment. The Laotians had little knowledge of Scripture or of Jesus. When Galli got to the passage where Jesus calms the storm, he asked the refugees to talk about the "storms" in their lives—their problems, worries, and struggles. The people looked confused and puzzled. Galli filled the awkward silence by asking, "So what are your storms?" Finally, one of the Laotian men asked, "Do you mean that Jesus actually calmed the wind and sea in the middle of a storm?" Galli thought the man was merely expressing his skepticism, and since he wasn't intending to spend the group's remaining time wrestling with the plausibility of Jesus' miracles, he said: "Yes, but we should not get hung up on the details of the miracle. We should remember that Jesus can calm the storms in our lives." After another uncomfortable stretch of silence, another man spoke up: "Well, if Jesus calmed the wind and the waves, he must be a very powerful man!" The Laotians buzzed with excitement about this while Galli looked on as a virtual outsider. While these newbie Christian refugees entered into something like worship, Galli realized he'd so taken Jesus for granted that he'd missed him altogether.[2]

In my own journey of awakening, I wondered whether I'd done the same thing as Galli. Had I so taken Jesus for granted in my life that I'd essentially stopped relating with him as he really is? Even more, had I so "understood" Jesus that the pursuit of him was far less interesting to me than the pursuit of Christian relationships or postmodern worship or artistic expressions of the Christian life or culturally relevant approaches to Bible study?

Now fast-forward a few more years from my personal deconstruction of WWJD. Last year I was invited to speak at a youth ministry conference in the Midwest. This time, my slot was a two-hour pre-conference session for people who wanted something a little deeper. At the time, I was experimenting with a training idea that focused all of youth ministry on three Jesus-centered questions:

2 Mark Galli, *Jesus Mean and Wild: The Unexpected Love of an Untamable God* (Grand Rapids, MI: Baker Books, 2006), p. 112.

1. "Who do I say Jesus is?"

Jesus asked his disciples this question after one of his huge public gatherings, when he'd gathered those closest to him to debrief the experience. This question was preceded by a safer one for the disciples: "Who do the people say I am?" Jesus, ever shrewd, tossed them an easy pitch to swing at before he brought the heat.

2. "Who does Jesus say I am?"

After Peter answered the first question by telling Jesus he was "the Christ, the son of the living God," Jesus fired back with his own answer to Peter's unasked question: "And you are Peter, whose real name is 'the Rock.'"

3. "Who do I say I am?"

Peter, after he betrayed his best friend, Jesus, had to answer the most important question of his life: "Am I the fake, duplicitous little man my betrayal is telling me I am, or am I the Rock Jesus told me I am?" After a little conference on the beach between Peter and the resurrected Jesus, when Jesus insisted on asking Peter *three times* if he loved him, the question is answered in Peter. You see his answer in the first two chapters of Acts as he stands before the crowds that only days before had demanded Jesus' crucifixion, and he *Rocks* them.

Later in this book I'll plunge more deeply into these three questions as crucial tunnels into Jesus-centered youth ministry. But for now it's merely important that you know where my head was at when I emerged from that two-hour training session. It was one of the most powerful worship experiences of my adult life because we'd sort of locked arms together and ran fast and hard after Jesus, not to get something from him, but just to *cling to him* as our primary youth ministry practice.

Now, because my training time happened before the conference had officially started, I had an open landscape before me to explore every nook and cranny hidden in the general sessions and workshops. I love that—sampling at the idea buffet and connecting with youth pastors who are the best, most enjoyable people I've ever known. But it didn't take long for the dissonance to set in. I was restless and, I had to admit, bored by almost everything I was hearing in the general sessions and workshops.

In truth, I was passionately bored.

These were some of the sharpest, most articulate and bold youth ministry veterans in the world. And I knew in my head that all the tips, techniques, and strategies they were dispensing were not only compelling but also practical. But the more I listened and tried to eat at their feast table, the blander their food looked to me.

Disillusioned, and suddenly feeling disconnected from the very people I'd looked forward to engaging, I found an empty seat in the large open space just outside of the conference room's doors. Thousands of people were swirling around me, but I felt like I was in a bubble. "Why, why, why, Jesus, am I feeling this way?" Tears welled in my eyes. I was literally pleading with him to shine His light on my sudden, unexpected darkness. And into that darkness I sensed him whispering: "You're bored by everything but me now."

What?

It's not that all the tips and techniques I'd been hearing were somehow contrary to a Jesus-centered youth ministry, any more than innovative cup holders are contrary to the Honda Odyssey my wife wishes we had. The cup holders are a nice, attractive addition, but you've got nothing without the drivetrain—the engine and transmission.

Now, I've spent a lot of time and creativity as editor of Group Magazine trying to point leaders toward the "cool cup holders" of youth ministry. As I've mentioned, I know I've unwittingly taken the "drivetrain" for granted in my life. As I sat there in my God bubble, I knew he was inviting me to obsess about Jesus like a "car person" obsesses about Hemi engines.

If a car is just of functional interest to you—something to get you from point A to point B—then its cup holders may weigh equally with the engine's specifications. But if you're a "car person"—someone who's fascinated and captivated by them— your primary passions are all about how it's propelled. A Web site for "muscle car" enthusiasts touts its drivetrain passion this way: "We have compiled one of the most extensive lists of block, crankshaft, and cylinder head casting numbers available on the internet. There are well over 20,000 listings here."[3] No mention of cup holders, but an obsessive focus on stuff related to the drivetrain.

In the midst of the conference's hubbub, it slowly dawned on me that my palpable boredom was the natural reaction of a "Jesus person"—I realized I'd slowly become obsessively interested only in youth ministry's "drivetrain." Somehow all of the workshops on relational ministry and postmodern worship and volunteer training—and all of the keynote speakers talking about creative processes and new youth ministry structures and axe-to-grind priorities—seemed like distractions from that thing rumbling under the hood. I felt like a "car person" at an auto show who's disappointed to learn that most of the workshops are about new windshield-wiper technologies and improved tread design for snow tires.

Frankly, this whole thing caught me by surprise, like stumbling into the Promised Land when I was only heading to 7-Eleven for a half gallon of milk. If a youth ministry of brilliant tips and techniques (cool cup holders) was now secondary to a youth ministry that is radically, creatively, passionately, uncomfortably centered around Jesus (the drivetrain), how would it change the way I see youth ministry? More important, how would it change what we *do* in youth ministry?

Well, obviously this book is my attempt at finding the way. And it would be arrogant of me—and a sort of betrayal of God's foundational commitment to relationship—to find the way using only the sonar of my own voice. So I've invited

---

3 From the www.musclecarclub.com home page.

the voices of youth pastors from all over the world, and of youth ministry friends and heroes, to join me in this adventure. And to the extent our voices resonate with your own, we've also captured your voice.

Now, let's see what it feels like when that engine is at full throttle.

Part One

THE
BEELINE
IMPERATIVE

The Spurgeon Way

The shadow cast by C. H. Spurgeon over this book is so broad it's not possible to go any further without exploring his life and mission a little first.

Spurgeon was a 19th-century English pastor who suffered from depression and a painful birth defect. He preached two services every Sunday in his London church, each with a crowd of 6,000 people attending (this was before the invention of microphones). At the time, he had more books in print than any other living person. He still has more books in print than any other pastor in history, including more than 2,500 of his published sermons. Historians call him the "Prince of Preachers," and his remarkable story holds the key to Jesus-centered youth ministry.

Spurgeon was born in England and committed his life to Christ in 1850, when he was 15 years old. He preached his first sermon a year later and took on the pastorate of a small Baptist church a year after that, at 17. Just four years after his conversion, the 20-year-old Spurgeon became pastor of London's famed New Park Street Chapel. A few months into his new position his skill and power as a preacher made him famous—at 22 he was the most popular preacher of the day.

Much later in Spurgeon's ministry, a young pastor asked him to listen to him preach and give him a critique—a common request since Spurgeon was revered by other preachers. After he listened to the young man's impassioned sermon, Spurgeon was honest—he thought it was well prepared and well delivered but it nevertheless...stunk.

"Will you tell me why you think it a poor sermon?" asked the young pastor.

"Because," said Spurgeon, "There was no Christ in it."

"If you think you can walk in holiness without keeping up perpetual fellowship with Christ, you have made a great mistake. If you would be holy, you must live close to Jesus."[1]

CHARLES HADDON SPURGEON

---

1 From an unedited sermon by Charles Haddon Spurgeon.

19

The young man said, "Well, Christ was not in the text; we are not to be preaching Christ always, we must preach what is in the text."

The old man responded, "Don't you know, young man, that from every town, and every village, and every little hamlet in England, wherever it may be, there is a road to London?"

"Yes," said the young man.

"Ah!" said the old preacher, "and so from *every text* in Scripture there is a road to the metropolis of the Scriptures, that is Christ. Dear brother, when you get to a text, say, 'Now, what is the road to Christ?' and then preach a sermon, running along the road towards the great metropolis—Christ."[2]

Spurgeon called this "making a beeline to Christ." It was his central, guiding commitment every time he opened his mouth to speak or teach or write.

He wrote: "Jesus is The Truth. We believe in Him—not merely in His words. He is the Doctor and the Doctrine, the Revealer and the Revelation, the Illuminator and the Light of Men. He is exalted in every word of truth, because he is its sum and substance. He sits above the gospel, like a prince on his own throne. Doctrine is most precious when we see it distilling from his lips and embodied in his person. Sermons are valuable in proportion as they speak of him and point to him. A Christless gospel is no gospel at all and a Christless discourse is the cause of merriment to devils."[3]

I believe Spurgeon's passion for Jesus, and his determination to track everything he said and did back to "the metropolis of Christ," is really the central—but unexplored—imperative in youth ministry today. What would a youth ministry look like that proactively found a beeline to Jesus for (literally) everything it did?

For example, instead of approaching Bible study or Bible teaching from a "life application" angle, we would use interesting topics—and every Bible passage—as the first step on a path toward Jesus. So no matter where we're studying in the Bible, or what topic we're studying, we always—*always*—find a beeline to Jesus.

This is no theoretical possibility; it's a practical reality. Let me show you what I mean.

Not long ago, I developed a series of youth ministry training events held in cities all over the country—it was called Group Magazine Live. At these events, we asked thousands of youth pastors to play with beeline Bible study. One person at each table closed his or her eyes, opened a Bible, and picked a random passage. Then, together with others at the table, the blind Bible stabber had just five minutes to identify the beeline to Christ from the random passage and put together a plan to teach that passage in a Jesus-centered way. (We gave them permission to use the "stabbed" verse in context with other verses.)

---

2 Taken from Sermon 242, *Christ Precious to Believers*, preached by Charles Spurgeon on March 13, 1859.

3 From the published sermons of Charles Haddon Spurgeon.

I always loved it when a table got "stuck" with something from Ezekiel or (horrors!) Leviticus. In *every single case* youth workers, who were, at first, as skeptical about the beeline as that young preacher had been, discovered the hidden beeline. Some groups were so excited about the experiment they chose to dive into the Bible a second time if they deemed their passage a "no-brainer" beeline.

The activity created a buzz of anticipation and even a sense of awe and worship. We followed that experience by challenging youth leaders to never again teach from the Bible, or plan a Bible study, or do a topical study of any kind, without making a beeline to Christ.

AND NOW FOR SOMETHING A LITTLE MORE RADICAL

I know "a beeline for everything" sounds radical, but we're in need of radical right now. Simply put, if what we're doing in youth ministry has no apparent connection to Jesus, then we ask God to help us find it.

In my example of Bible study, it's good to remember that John's gospel tells us Jesus is "the Word"—meaning his fingerprints are all over the Bible. There's a built-in beeline to Jesus no matter where you go in Scripture. It's our imperative (and a grand, playful adventure) to find it.

I'm going to try again, right now, to experiment with this while you watch (read). Ready? Here we go.

First I close my eyes, and then I stab my finger into my Bible and come

DANGER OF IRRELEVANCE?

If we're always making a beeline to Jesus, what do we do about the issues—the problems and challenges—facing our teenagers? Drug and alcohol abuse? Sexual activity? The push to succeed? Divorce? Depression? Stress? Cultural influences? This is exactly the issue the young preacher, flabbergasted and annoyed, was targeting when he told Spurgeon: "We are not to be preaching Christ always, we must preach what is in the text."

Up until now most of us have been like overworked pruners in a fast-growing orchard. We scurry around trying to cut off the bad fruit we see around us. We do teaching series on sex, on money, on music and movies, on relationships…The truth is, as kids come to know Jesus more deeply and begin to abide in him as the "root" of their life, their fruit will change. They will be transformed "by the renewing of [their] mind" (Romans 12:2). We won't have to run around cutting off rotten fruit!

But that's not to say we won't need to focus on these topics—we'll just focus on them with the goal of helping kids find and experience the beeline to Jesus.

up with Job 5:22—it's in the middle of a speech by Eliphaz (one of Job's "friends") titled "The Innocent Do Not Suffer." The "advice" that encompasses verse 22 actually starts in verse 17:

> "Blessed is the man whom God corrects; so do not despise the discipline of the Almighty. For he wounds, but he also binds up; he injures, but his hands also heal. From six calamities he will rescue you; in seven no harm will befall you. In famine he will ransom you from death, and in battle from the stroke of the sword. You will be protected from the lash of the tongue, and need not fear when destruction comes. [Verse 22] You will laugh at destruction and famine, and need not fear the beasts of the earth."

So I close my eyes again and pray: *God, where is the beeline?* In a moment, I have it (I'm sure there are many more ways to go with this, but this is the one that surfaces for me in this moment): I would use this passage for a study or teaching titled "What Does Jesus *Really* Promise Us?" I'd compare Eliphaz's view of a God who punishes the bad and rewards the good to Jesus' mission to love even his enemies. And I'd scan the gospels to pluck out every promise Jesus made and compare them to what Eliphaz *represents* as God's promises. That's the beeline—I'd attach everything in the study to it, and I'd use personal interactions, experiences, and relevant stories plucked from mainstream media (film, music, or video games).

As I mentioned, we've now trained thousands of youth pastors to do what I just did. The effect of finding the beeline in everything we do, all the time, is that the truth Spurgeon discovered—that all roads lead to the metropolis of Christ—gets injected into kids' spiritual DNA. It changes forever the way they view Scripture study, mission trips, service projects, games, retreats, and (most importantly) their everyday lives. And it will flip a switch in them that can't be turned off, one that enables them to find Jesus—or the kingdom of God he describes—everywhere they look.

SPURGEON THE YOUTH PASTOR

Not long ago I experimented with the beeline by crafting a commitment statement that would drive everything I do with Group Magazine. Here's what I came up with:

> *We believe that youth ministries have slowly, imperceptibly shifted their focus from Jesus as the center of all our ministry activities to lesser goals. We assert that Jesus is the obvious and persistent focus of effective youth ministries. And we believe that youth pastors have maximum impact, in partnership with God, when they work to connect everything they do back to Jesus.*

I think this commitment statement well reflects the sharp turn we need to make in youth ministry—that's why I think Spurgeon would make a great youth pastor in today's climate. He was scorned by the "Pharisees" of his time for being too "proletariat"—he spoke to the masses and was popular with working people. That's because his message was simple, simple, simple: "A sermon without Christ as its beginning, middle, and end is a mistake in conception and a crime in execution."[4]

Spurgeon's simple beeline focus is really the only pillar strong enough to serve as the central weight-bearing support for any and all ministry strategies—purpose-driven ministry, family ministry, relational ministry, postmodern/emergent ministry—anything. In fact, you can see this "pillar" propping up the most effective youth ministries in America—the passionate, consuming pursuit of Jesus is a common thread woven through their diverse structures, locations, and challenges.

In the groundbreaking *Study of Exemplary Congregations in Youth Ministry*,[5] researchers found that central pillar and named it—a single-minded, persistent, saturating focus on Jesus Christ. The three-year study combined quantitative research with qualitative insights drawn from intensive site visits to the targeted youth ministries. They focused on churches in seven major denominations that had become known within their circles as "exemplary"—profoundly "successful in shaping the faith lives of youth."

Pastors and youth pastors connected to exemplary youth ministries were asked to complete this sentence: "The youth ministry of our congregation would die if..." The common response was: "If the ministry's emphasis shifts away from its focus on Jesus Christ." These ministries are kindred spirits to the apostle Paul, who condensed his life's ambitions into one sentence in 1 Corinthians 2:2: "For I determined to know nothing among you except Jesus Christ, and Him crucified" (NASB). Can that statement be the simple driving force, the hub, of a youth ministry?

I think it must be.

In this book I'll sprinkle examples, comments, and ideas drawn from the exemplary youth ministries in the study—to flesh out what it looks like to live out a beeline focus in every area of ministry. These ministries are organized like a bicycle wheel—where the hub is Jesus and the spokes are all the events, programs, practices, and activities of the ministry. Here's what I mean:

---

4 From the published sermons of Charles Haddon Spurgeon, 1625.598.

5 To learn more about the *Study of Exemplary Congregations in Youth Ministry*, go to www.exemplarym.com. The quotes from youth pastors, adult volunteers, senior pastors, and teenagers cited in the study throughout this book are taken from the study's in-site interviews.

The common pursuit of these exemplary youth ministries is summed up by an adult volunteer at Rochester Covenant Church in Minnesota, one of the churches in the study: "The genius [of our youth ministry] is a passion for Christ, everything else just falls into place."

And that sounds like the biggest taken-for-granted truth in youth ministry, doesn't it? *Of course* Jesus is at the center of everything we do. As I talk about this around the country, that's often the first reaction I get. But that's before I pull up my dump truck of "evidence" and unload it on them (perhaps a poor choice of metaphors there, but nevertheless...).

If our great-great-grandfather Spurgeon could roll over in his grave, that's what he'd be doing right now. The beeline he imbedded into everything he did is simply missing from so much of youth ministry today. I'll start my exploration into the "evidence" through the portal of my own journey from a "just add Jesus" recipe for effective youth ministry to a "Jesus alone" recipe.

This Changes Everything

've lived in Colorado for most of my life, so it's easy to take the Rocky Mountains for granted. I know that's hard to believe because people come from all over the world to enjoy the wild, craggy beauty of these mountains. In fact, if I were to turn my head right now I could see them just outside of my window...but I'm busy writing this so I won't.

Often, when I'm lugging my laptop and my briefcase and my big U.S. Postal Service bin (that I'm not supposed to have) full of books and papers and videotapes and other stuff into my office in the morning, I sense God nudging me, caffeinating my soul, stopping me in my tracks. Here's a loose translation of what surfaces inside me when I pause to listen:

"Rick, take your eyes off the asphalt. Look up. Stop. Smell the air. No, don't sniff it—drink it in. Suck it down to the bottom of your lungs. And while those sweet smells of the Rocky Mountain West rush through your mouth and nostrils, let your eyes rest for a moment on my beauty. Yeah, those mountains are literally close enough to touch, aren't they? If you were 47 percent more rebellious you'd drop everything right now and just walk into the mountains to find a stream to sit by for the day. Remember where you are, Rick. Remember what your life is really all about. Remember who I am—I'm the chief purveyor of 'useless beauty,' to quote my unknowing prophet Elvis Costello."

Honestly, he says something just like this to me...only *slightly* embellished by my overactive embellisher, no doubt. And then I let out a little sigh, glance back one more time, wave my name badge in front of the card reader, and walk

> "And that's really the most surprising thing about life— it really takes very little for me to forget about Jesus."

through the door into the land of responsibility—of course, that door is also a diving board that launches me into the grand adventure of my calling. I don't think God is telling me I'll find my life in the slipstream of Ferris Bueller. I think he's reminding me to remember him. The sigh, I think, is a tiny little lament for how easy it is for me to succumb to the responsibilities and details of my life and forget the greater truths that literally overshadow me. I live in one of the world's most beautiful places—the late-afternoon shadows that creep across the parking lot at Group Publishing are mountain-shaped. I love...love everything about the West.

But something so much greater, something more beautiful and wild, overshadows me—his name is Jesus. Every moment of beauty and meaning and purpose I've ever experienced in life is shot through with him. I love the extravagantly careless way he throws beauty around. But more than that I love Jesus himself—his sweet, sweet smell fills my nostrils and sinks to my depths... when I'm not staring at the asphalt of my life.

And that's really the most surprising thing about life—it really takes very little for me to forget about him. You'd *think* my metaphorical asphalt was more interesting to me because I forget—*I forget*—to remember the beauty that looms over me. And it's just as possible to forget about Jesus as it is to forget about the Rocky Mountains. I feel perfectly at peace admitting this because I'm in the company of those millions (billions?) before me who inexplicably but most certainly forgot all about Jesus while they were busy inviting others into his kingdom.

MISSING JESUS

In his book *Following Jesus*, the great British theologian N. T. Wright says, "The longer you look at Jesus, the more you will want to serve him. That is of course, if it's the real Jesus you're looking at."[1] Wright is saying that it's very possible for us to miss the shadow cast by the real Jesus—that we can simply overlook his looming presence, that we can literally forget who he *really* is. Instead, we end up following a guy who *looks* a lot like Jesus but is actually more like the longhaired guy who makes your sub sandwich—polite, eager to serve, helpful, and comfortably anonymous.

Remember my hopscotch through the gospel of Matthew back in the Introduction? The last Jesus truth I pulled from that experiment was: "Our biggest faith battle is remembering to remember God."

I think "Remembering Jesus" is the key to a life of faithfulness. That's too bad, because we're all world-class forgetters, no matter how good we are at keeping track of our PINs and computer passwords. If you look at the people of God throughout history, you'll see they move through a remarkably predictable cycle—they stray from God, God disciplines, the people remember God, they return to faithfulness, they start forgetting, they stray...and the cycle repeats

---

1 N. T. Wright, *Following Jesus: Biblical Reflections on Discipleship* (Grand Rapids, MI: Eerdmans, 1994), p. ix.

again and again. (For a microcosm of the cycle, look no further than the book of Exodus.) It's happening right now, in our culture, this very moment in our youth ministries, maybe even with you personally. Certainly with me.

When I began to notice this cycle surfacing in Scripture, in history, in American culture, and in my own life, I laid two questions on God's table:

1. Is this cycle a given—am I destined to repeat its painful revolution over and over in my life?
2. And if not, what will vault me out of the cycle?

I believe God answered my two questions this way:

1. No.
2. Remember to remember me.

This sparked in me a desire to pursue, to discover, what it means to proactively *remember* God in my everyday life. How can remembering Jesus be as autonomic as breathing to me?

It's God's Holy Spirit who does this kind of work and transformation. He takes the lead in Genesis 9:15: "I will *remember* my covenant between me and you and all living creatures of every kind."

In the light (and safety) of that promise, he does what any good father would do—he asks us to shoulder our responsibility in 1 Chronicles 16:11-13: "Look to the Lord and his strength; seek his face always. *Remember* the wonders he has done, his miracles, and the judgments he pronounced, O descendants of Israel his servant, O sons of Jacob, his chosen ones."

Finally, he trains his followers to pass on the thread of remembering, weaving it into the lives of those God is raising up in his name. That's why Paul, in his old age, gave Timothy this bit of parting advice in 2 Timothy 2:8-9: "*Remember* Jesus Christ, raised from the dead, descended from David. This is my gospel, for which I am suffering even to the point of being chained like a criminal."

Now Paul was imprisoned because of his aggressive pursuit of Jesus, and Timothy had lived through beatings and shipwrecks and imprisonments with him—all for the glory and honor of Jesus. Why would Paul have to *remind* Timothy about Jesus? I think it was because he was humble enough to admit the truth— everyone, including Paul, Timothy, John the Baptist, Peter, and the disciples... and now you and me...are notorious forgetters.

SO CLOSE, SO FAR AWAY

The point is this—our *remembering* is central to God's mission on earth. That means *forgetting* is our greatest enemy, and there's never a time riper for seducing us into forgetting than when we're pretty comfortable in our understanding of

Jesus. And that time is *this time*—we're way, way too comfortable and satisfied in our knowledge and understanding of Jesus.

Just last week I was listening to a well-known church consultant talk about cultural trends that are having an impact on the church today. I heard lots of facts and illustrations about "top down" versus "bottom up," "dictatorial" versus "participatory," "isolating" versus "connecting," "big box" versus "intimate space," and so on.

And then my drivetrain obsession kicked in.

I realized the church consultant was *only* exploring horizontal issues—I mean, issues about the way we help young people experience church and Christian fellowship. To me, it was a very, very interesting discussion about cup holders. And I realized that almost all the very, very interesting discussions and movements in youth ministry today are about cup holders—that's why I was so bored at the conference where my "God bubble" experience happened.

So I raised my hand to ask the church consultant: "I'd like to throw out to you my own little 'axe to grind' and get your response—everything you're talking about is very interesting but very horizontal to me, so where does the pursuit of Jesus fit into all of this?"

The consultant looked at me for an uncomfortably long moment—it was a mini-cliffhanger in an otherwise easy stroll through the church jungle, so everyone else was waiting there at the cliff's edge for the consultant to respond.

"Well, of course, we can't forget the story in all of this," the consultant said, finally. "In the midst of changing and adapting our ministries to meet the challenges of a rapidly changing culture, we have to hang on to what we've always known." The consultant went on in this vein for a few more minutes and then was clearly ready to move on.

So I raised my hand again and said: "Actually, I don't think it's a good idea at all to 'hang on to what we know'—I think we're now at a place where we're so comfortable with Jesus, so confident of who he is and what he's like, that a lot of 'what we know' is actually *wrong*. We've kind of lost interest in him, like a married couple in midlife. We think we pretty much have him pegged—all the things we like and all the things that have been bugging us about him for years. We've been married a long time to Jesus and gone through a lot together. But one of the marriage partners—the church—is sort of looking around for something to spark our passions because we're past the 'passionate curiosity' stage with Jesus. So we turn to the 'form and function' of doing church as our mid-marriage splurge— like buying a little red sports car to rouse us from our relational boredom (some postmodern worship ideas, for example). If we're not awake to this dynamic, our 'marriage' could descend into deadness and a sense of growing isolation—we'll literally live under the same roof with Jesus but live separate lives, functionally apart from him."

When I was finished with my diatribe, I couldn't tell whether the consultant was intrigued by what I was saying or patiently waiting for me to close my mouth so we could move back to the agenda at hand. But our little interchange had created a stir in the group—several people excitedly stopped me at the break. I'd smeared a little mud in their eyes, just like Greg Stier had done for me. One of them said, "What all people—young and old—are *really* hungry for today is Jesus." We stared at each other a little awkwardly, smiling and staunch like the hobbits in the *Fellowship of the Ring*. Our brief, energetic conversation was a form of worship in that moment.

THE JESUS-SHAPED HOLE IN YOUTH MINISTRY

David and Kelli Trujillo are contributing editors for Group Magazine. Not long ago they sent me another set of Bible studies for the magazine—imbedded in one of them was a quiz game that plunges teenagers into the dangers of this mid-marriage dynamic. First, you have kids play a quiz game that focuses on American slang words. You throw out a slang word to them and give them multiple definitions to choose from. For example, here are some slang words and their definitions from the *Dictionary of American Slang*:

SLANG TERM	DEFINITION
cabbage	money
skillion	a ridiculously large number
refrigerator	prison
the man	the establishment
the cat's meow	someone remarkable
swank	stylish
lame duck	an irresponsible or weak person

After the game, you offer kids this slang sentence and see if they can translate it: "I know you itch a mean ivory so I'll be on the gitbox here and you hit the eighty-eights, and we'll clef a humdinger." *(Translation: "You can play the piano very well, so I'll play the guitar and you play the piano and we'll compose an exceedingly great song.")*

Next, you throw them a harder one: "That sockdolaging wing-waiter of mine is tipping grand." *(Translation: "That great man, who is my mail carrier, is walking fast.")*

Then, say David and Kelli, you drive home the point: Sometimes we miss the meaning of something because we're not familiar with the terms, but sometimes we miss the meaning of a word, or at the very least miss the impact of a word, because we're *too* familiar with it.[2] That word is *Jesus*. We're that older married

---

2 From "Bible Studies," by David and Kelli Trujillo, Group Magazine, November/December 2006.

couple heading toward a divorce because we're functionally arrogant in our self-satisfied knowledge of our spouse. Actually, a deep threat to youth ministry's "marriage" relationship with Jesus wouldn't be a bad thing. When you're about to lose what's most important to you because of bored neglect, you have a crucial chance to see your "spouse" with new eyes.

Of course, in today's youth ministry, I'm saying we're in need of a near-divorce experience—both personally and as a body—to reawaken our wonder and passionate pursuit of Jesus.

Donald Miller, author of *Searching for God Knows What*, says he once conducted an experiment in a Bible college class he was teaching—he told his students he was going to explain the basics of the gospel message to them but leave out one crucial truth. He challenged them to pick out the missing truth. He proceeded to conduct the experiment by talking about man's sinfulness and examples of depravity in our culture, our need to repent because the wages of sin is death, the beauty of morality and the great hope of heaven, and all the great things we can experience once we're saved from the consequences of our sin.

In Miller's class, not a single one of his Bible-college-educated students pointed out that "Jesus" was the missing "crucial truth." Miller writes: "I presented a gospel to Christian Bible college students and left out Jesus. Nobody noticed...[3]"

Of course, Miller's students are *not* the exception to the rule. Many in youth ministry are already pretty certain we've got the whole Jesus-centered thing covered.

Not long ago I was listening to a nationally known youth ministry speaker as he led a large room of eager youth leaders through a training workshop. He told how a youth worker had come up to him during a break. This guy said to him, "You know, all your tips and advice are fine, but aren't we supposed to be focusing on Jesus in youth ministry?" The speaker smiled and told the crowd how he'd responded to the guy: "Of course youth ministry is about Jesus—c'mon, that's a given." That produced a lot of smiling, nodding heads in the crowd.

Like the church consultant encounter I've already described, this story made me squirm in my seat.

And we should all be squirming in our seats, because we have the evidence—both hard and soft—that proves this youth ministry veteran and the church consultant are missing something big about our greatest youth ministry need. In the next chapter I'll serve up a heaping plate of hard evidence. But before we get to the stats and research, here's a crucial piece of "soft evidence" that I haven't yet shared with you. Greg Stier's little Spurgeon mud treatment brought everything into clear focus for me, but something else had already profoundly prepared me to see the light.

---

3 Donald Miller, *Searching for God Knows What* (Nashville, TN, Thomas Nelson, 2004) pp. 157-159.

THE CARDIGAN JESUS

A little over a year ago, I was talking with a junior high girl who'd just served as a leader in a churchwide worship experience during Holy Week. This girl had spent several days leading people from her congregation into a deeper relationship with Jesus through an interactive devotional experience. She was giddy with excitement about the whole thing. I told her I'd been asking teenagers to describe Jesus to me...just because I was curious.

"So," I asked, "what are some words you'd use to describe Jesus to someone who's never heard of him?"

She thought, and then thought some more. Then she edged her way into a hopeful response: "Well, I'd have to say he's really, really nice."

I waited for more, but there was no more. So I asked, "Remember that time Jesus made a whip and chased all the moneychangers out of the temple? Does that story change the way you describe Jesus?"

She thought and thought and thought. Finally, with the tone of someone raising a white flag over a crumbling wall, she said, "Well, I know Jesus is nice, so what he did must have been nice."

I nodded and smiled grimly.

I was both disturbed and intrigued by this experience. So I decided to ask teenagers all over the country the same question—what do they really know about Jesus, and how do they expect him to act? We hired video crews and asked them to stop kids randomly on the street and ask them a simple question: "How would you describe Jesus?"

When I got all the raw footage back, I discovered my experience with the junior high girl was not an aberration. Without fail, teenagers' first and favorite descriptive word for Jesus was always "nice." Here's a tiny sampler of their comments:

- "I'd describe Jesus as a nice, friendly guy."
- "[He's] a very nice, caring guy."
- "He's, um, nice."
- "Umm....[he's] very nice?"
- "He was a good person."
- "He's a nice, friendly person."[4]

These comments were profoundly sad for me. It's the same way I'd feel if someone, not knowing that I'm married to my wife, Bev, told me that the best thing about her is that she's incredibly...tidy. Sure, Jesus was nice when he healed people and when he invited children to sit on his lap. But he was definitely not nice when he was blasting (over and over) religious leaders or calling his lead disciple "Satan" or when he told the rich young ruler to sell all his possessions

---

4 From the raw footage of videotaped interviews of teenagers across America, in 2005.

and follow him if that ruler wanted to "inherit eternal life." In Matthew 23 he told the Pharisees they were "hopeless"—not once, but *seven times* in a row—and then he put the cherry on the top of that poisonous sundae by calling them "manicured grave plots," "total frauds," and "snakes" (from *The Message*). In Luke 11:37-45, the good doctor Luke relates this often-overlooked little lightning bolt about Jesus—as you read, think how you'd feel if you were a church leader who'd graciously invited an itinerant preacher to have dinner with your family:

> When Jesus had finished speaking, a Pharisee invited him to eat with him; so he went in and reclined at the table. But the Pharisee, noticing that Jesus did not first wash before the meal, was surprised. Then the Lord said to him, "Now then, you Pharisees clean the outside of the cup and dish, but inside you are full of greed and wickedness. You foolish people! Did not the one who made the outside make the inside also? But give what is inside the dish to the poor, and everything will be clean for you.
>
> "Woe to you Pharisees, because you give God a tenth of your mint, rue and all other kinds of garden herbs, but you neglect justice and the love of God. You should have practiced the latter without leaving the former undone. Woe to you Pharisees, because you love the most important seats in the synagogues and greetings in the marketplaces. Woe to you, because you are like unmarked graves, which men walk over without knowing it."
>
> One of the experts in the law answered him, "Teacher, when you say these things, you insult us also."

I can just imagine this scene—you're not even eating dinner yet when your invited guest suddenly wipes the polite smile off your face by repeatedly insulting you. Then, still managing to respond politely and trying to give your guest the benefit of the doubt, you innocently ask him if he's aware that he's insulting you. Jesus picks up after verse 45 by effectively saying, "Yes, I'm aware I'm insulting you, and I'm only just getting started."

The point is that a *merely* nice Jesus is no Jesus at all—he's like a declawed version of Narnia's Aslan. And here's the really important thing: A declawed Jesus is not strong and fierce and *big* enough to walk with kids (or us) into the fiery furnaces of their everyday life. They're facing big challenges and struggles, and they're looking for someone or something that can help them through or make them forget all about their troubles. Mr. Rogers is a pleasant enough guy, but you wouldn't follow him into a dark alley full of street thugs waiting to beat you up. Because "nice Jesus" doesn't seem able to enter into the dark alleys in kids' lives, they naturally turn to other "gods," including:

- drugs and alcohol
- video games
- sexual experimentation
- spirituality

- sports
- discipline and self-empowerment
- their own untapped "potential"

During my long sojourn as editor of Group Magazine, youth ministry experts, resource providers, trainers, and other barnacles (including me!) have tried to direct youth ministry's focus toward cool cup holders—student-led ministry, family ministry, relational ministry, postmodern ministry, and anti-Chubby Bunny ministry. It wasn't until God connected my WWJD deconstruction with "nice Jesus" and my "God bubble" experience and Greg Stier's Spurgeon mudpack that I realized how profoundly we'd been overlooking the elephant in the living room—his name is Jesus.

It's clear that despite our best efforts—all our training, commitment, resources, and creativity—today's teenagers are just not getting who Jesus really is, or they're not getting *enough* of who he really is, or they're getting, literally, a fake Jesus. As a result, few of them are living passionately with Christ in their everyday life.

Could it be it's not just the church that's in the middle of mid-marriage boredom with Jesus, but it's us—you and me—too?

The point of this book is to explore together how a *Jesus-centered life* can lead to a *Jesus-centered youth ministry*. I'm convinced that we'll recover our own life and our youth ministry vision and practice when we, like Spurgeon, return to the center of all things:

Jesus Christ.

Do We Know What We Think We Know?

A few years ago I got a call out of the blue from Dr. Christian Smith, at the time a professor of sociology at the University of North Carolina at Chapel Hill (he's now at Notre Dame). We'd never met. Chris was calling to ask if I'd consider serving on the public advisory board for a major new study he was leading that targeted teenagers' religious beliefs and behaviors. He'd gotten my name from a mutual friend who'd already been invited onto the advisory board. I'd never done anything like this, but he was basically offering to pay me to sit around a table with a wide array of interesting people and spout my opinions about teenagers, youth culture, and youth ministry. I got off the phone and told my wife, "I can do that in my sleep."

Well, that ridiculously easy "yes" plunged me into one of the most satisfying experiences of my life. I got an intimate insider's view of the *National Study of Youth and Religion*[1]—the best and broadest exploration of teenagers' faith beliefs and practices that has ever been done. Chris and his team accomplished what no one before had attempted—a comprehensive sketch of what kids believe and how they live out those beliefs. They conducted extensive phone interviews with more than 3,000 young people and then interviewed one parent in each of those homes. Then they sampled from that

> "Kids essentially see God as a 'divine butler' or a 'cosmic therapist'— Jesus' job is to help them do what they want, make them happy, and solve their problems."

---

[1] To learn more about the *National Study of Youth and Religion*, go to www.youthandreligion.com or pick up Smith's book (with Melinda Lundquist Denton) *Soul Searching: The Religious and Spiritual Lives of American Teenagers* (New York: Oxford University Press, 2005).

pool and did half-day, face-to-face interviews with about 300 teenagers to flesh out the answers to their phone-interview questions. Chris and his researchers produced a looming mountain of data, stories, and personal experiences with teenagers all over America.

The results of the study were released in Chris' book (with Melinda Lundquist Denton) *Soul Searching: The Religious and Spiritual Lives of American Teenagers* (Oxford University Press), and I took a whack at interpreting the study's results for youth ministry in the book *Youth Ministry in the 21st Century* (Group Publishing).

The study found that a "hub" relationship with Jesus is far down the list of teenagers' priorities. Instead, Chris found that kids essentially see God as a "divine butler" or a "cosmic therapist"—Jesus' job is to help them do what they want, make them happy, and solve their problems.

In fact, the Jesus today's kids believe in behaves a lot like a well-known TV icon from the '70s—Mr. Roarke from *Fantasy Island*. If you've never seen this campy, sentimental, and wildly popular relic from the disco age, here's a thumbnail description of the show.

Mr. Roarke, played by the ever-suave Ricardo Montalban, was something like the ageless king of Fantasy Island. He always wore white, was older but had a youthful personality, and was almost always smooth, encouraging, and nice. But he could be stern—especially with people who were trying to trick him or who had bad motives. *He existed to make the dreams of good people come true.* You couldn't really know him—watching the show you never learn anything about his private life or what drives him. He was powerful but distant. If you stayed on his good side, things were OK. He even had a strange-looking little helper who dressed in *angelic* white.

If you condense the results of the National Study of Youth and Religion, *you realize that Mr. Roarke is exactly how teenagers see Jesus.*

JESUS, WE NEVER KNEW YOU

In a survey several years ago, Christian pollster George Barna proclaimed that many Christian teenagers are ignorant about basic faith beliefs. In the past, I've objected (in the pages of Group Magazine) to some of Barna's conclusions about young people and youth ministry. So I decided to replicate his study by asking more than 10,000 Christian kids participating in our summer workcamp program essentially the same questions, plus a few more. After compiling the results, we found a brighter picture than Barna painted, but still confirmed many of his core findings. Here's how these Christian kids answered two key questions:

• *About four out of 10 (38 percent) say a good person can earn eternal salvation through good deeds.*

This is a commonly held belief that negates the very nature and mission of Christ—it makes his sacrifice on the cross just another irrelevant blip in a history book. When the rich young ruler approached Jesus to ask him a question (Luke 18:18-19), the young man started by addressing him as "good teacher" and then asked what good thing he had to do to inherit eternal life. At first Jesus ignored the man's question and zeroed in on the way that he'd greeted him: " 'Why do you call me good?' Jesus answered. 'No one is good—except God alone.' " Jesus was shrewdly emphasizing a powerful truth—no one is good except…him. And the more you know Jesus, the more this truth is self-evident. The fact that so many Christian kids believe *their goodness* will save them reveals how little they understand Jesus for who he really is.

• *Almost a quarter of Christian teens (22 percent) say Jesus committed sins while he lived on earth.*

Of course, if Jesus committed sins—any sin—our salvation is a vapor. I think this response is much more about kids' utter immersion in a world of sin. After all, one episode of *Desperate Housewives* or the *House of Carters* or *Survivor* is enough to convince you that sinning is a given—no one can escape its pull. In teen logic, that means even Jesus was susceptible to sin.

How could so many churchgoing teenagers miss the basic truths of Christianity? How could they not understand that they simply aren't "good" enough to earn their own salvation—that Jesus is God incarnate and therefore sinless in the totality of his life on earth and beyond? Could it be these kids never learned some of these important truths at church?

Well, our survey results found that the number of kids who say they've learned "Jesus is God" at church is an overwhelming 87 percent.[2] The truth between the lines here is a mixture of three problems, I think:

1. A lot of teenagers are learning the "right answers" about Jesus at church and home, but they're barely getting a whiff of who he *really* is at church and at home.

2. The few kids who are getting a healthy exposure to the true Jesus are subjugating him to their preconceived, mistaken notions—"When Jesus cleared the temple that must have been a nice thing because Jesus is nice."

3. They see pretty clearly that *we think* Jesus is God, but they're not experiencing how "saturating" our relationship with him is—how he spills into every aspect of our lives, how he's no declawed Aslan or boring partner in a too-comfortable marriage.

At times I've criticized Christian musicians for writing Roarke-ian lyrics about Jesus and the Christian life (more on this in a later chapter). So much

---

2 All results from a Group Publishing survey of more than 10,000 Christian teenagers attending a Group workcamp in the summer of 2001—the survey was titled *Back to the Basics.*

of today's contemporary Christian music fuels the prevailing falsehoods about who Jesus is and what he came to do. That's why I was a little stunned to read a Christian musician skewer the Roarke-ian Christian life with amazing power and clarity. In a little sidebar to a CCM Magazine feature on the hard music band Underoath, one of the band's guitarists, Tim McTague, wrote:

> I believe that we, as "Christians," have lost sight of what Christ intended our lives to be and the purpose and faith He gave His life to teach us. As long as we give our 39 cents a day and make it to church on Wednesday and Sunday, we're all good...the American way...the new "Christianity." Whatever happened to the church of Acts where people would sell all they had and give to the poor and join a body of thousands of people, living a life of prayer, community and servanthood?
>
> We now sit, 2,000 years later, in our comfortable homes and Lexuses and mega-church youth groups watching the rest of the world rot away and starve to death. Where is Christ in our watered down, self-serving hybrid of faith and hypocrisy...the new "Christianity"? God exists to pay our mortgages and heal our families, but, when it comes time to sacrifice something of our own, we look away. We're too concerned with church attendance and having the biggest building in town to see that we're wasting our days and God's money for our own comfort and well-being. The answer to our world's issues isn't charity drives and new taxes and Republican parties...but, rather, a complete renewal of thinking. Loving people as you would want to be loved, clothing the cold, feeding the hungry and housing the homeless—not at God's expense but our own—giving all we have in order to shine the light of Christ and live a life that counts.
>
> Somewhere along the way, we decided that being a Christian wasn't a life of serving but a life of being served. I can't change anything with 400 words...but you can change the world. God is real and is waiting for a few real Christians to step up and let Him work through them the way He worked through the disciples. But it will cost everything...This is no longer YOUR life...so stop living like it is. God have mercy on us all.[3]

Wow, that's some blistering stuff. But the *National Study of Youth and Religion* undergirds everything McTague writes. According to the NSYR, most American young people believe that

---

3 From a sidebar titled "Whose Life Is It Anyway?" by Tim McTague, in the July 2006 issue of CCM Magazine.

- God exists, that this being created and orders the world and watches over human life on earth.
- this God wants people to be good, nice, and fair to each other—as taught in the Bible and by most world religions.
- the central goal of life is to be happy and to feel good about yourself.
- God does not need to be particularly involved in your life, except when you need God to resolve a problem.
- good people go to heaven when they die.
- church is just another thing on a list of things to do—it's not where they enjoy their closest friendships.

This list of functional beliefs offers no evidence that young people have had a close encounter with the Jesus described by the gospel writers. In his foreword to Mark Galli's book *Jesus Mean and Wild*, Eugene Peterson writes: "Every omitted detail of Jesus, so carefully conveyed to us by the Gospel writers, reduces Jesus. We need the whole Jesus. The complete Jesus. Everything he said. Every detail of what He did."[4]

I love the scene from one of the Narnia books—*The Voyage of the Dawn Treader*—when the bratty, self-centered boy Eustace suddenly finds himself magically turned into a terrible, ugly dragon after he discovers an abandoned pile of dragon treasure and falls into a greedy sleep. At first the noxious boy enjoys the fear he can now produce in people as he swoops at them, breathing fire. But soon he's lonely, afraid, and miserable as a dragon. And his arm is really hurting because he slipped a dragon-treasure bracelet onto his wrist before he fell asleep and now it's constricting his much larger dragon limb. In the midst of his misery, a large fearsome lion (Aslan) comes to him in the night—he's afraid of the lion but not afraid of it eating him. It's a different kind of fear—the kind you feel when you're in the presence of someone much bigger and greater than you.

Anyway, the lion leads Eustace to a well in the mountains and tells him he must "undress" before he slips into the well's soothing waters. Eustace doesn't understand what it means to "undress" at first because he's, well, already a naked dragon. But soon he figures out that he should try to tear away at his dragon skin to see if he can find the boy still living underneath it. He does this three times, to no effect. Then the lion says: "You will have to let me undress you." Because Eustace is desperate, he lies on his dragon back and exposes his soft underbelly to the lion's claws: "The first tear he made was so deep that I thought it had gone right into my heart," he says. And after the lion tears away the deepest remnants of Eustace's dragon skin, he invites him into the water. When he emerges he's a boy again (actually, a boy redeemed), soon to be dressed in "new clothes" by the lion, who is Jesus Christ in full.[5]

4 Eugene Peterson, from the foreword for *Jesus Mean and Wild: The Unexpected Love of an Untamable God* by Mark Galli (Grand Rapids, MI: Baker Books), p. 11.

5 C. S. Lewis, *The Voyage of the Dawn Treader* (New York: Macmillan, 1970), pp. 88-91.

A SPOKE ON THE WHEEL

If the teenagers profiled in the *National Study of Youth and Religion* had really met the Jesus depicted in Lewis' story, their responses to the researchers would've been radically different. He's no "divine butler" or "cosmic therapist"—more like the "divine tornado" or the "cosmic William Wallace," the heroic Scottish rescuer of the poor and oppressed depicted in Mel Gibson's film *Braveheart*.

In my mind, the key finding of the study is that just one out of 10 American young people have what NSYR researchers call a "devoted" faith—that means, for nine out of 10 kids,

- their faith in Christ is not central to their life.
- they don't know the basics of their faith.
- they don't see how their relationship with Jesus makes an impact in their everyday life.[6]

For almost all teenagers, Jesus is not the hub of their life—he's either a "spoke" on their life's wheel (just a church thing) or not even part of the wheel. They have no firm idea of who Jesus really is, why he came, what he actually said, what he actually did, or what he's doing now. And when something happens in their "real" world, they struggle to understand God's connection to it.

Just after the devastating Indonesian tsunami in 2004 claimed more than 200,000 lives, *World News Tonight* did a special report on the religious response to the tragedy. The reporter interviewed representatives from every major world religion, including a professor of Christian theology. The big question the report was trying to answer was: "Where was God in this tragedy?" Implied in that question is another one: "Who is God and what does he do?"

These are huge, everyday questions for teenagers—they want to know what role God can or will play in their own life crises. They want to know what he'll do when they're hurting or scared or needy. And after the tsunami they wanted to know what God was doing while all those innocents—including helpless little babies—drowned. But the answers they heard (if they were watching *World News Tonight* that evening) were appallingly shallow. They heard Buddhist leaders say the tsunami happened so the victims could reincarnate into a better position in life. They heard Muslim leaders say the victims won an opportunity to be vaulted into a higher "level" of heaven. And they heard Christian leaders say the worst natural disaster in modern history was merely a backdrop for the later response of compassion.[7]

They heard nothing that would help them understand God as he really is. In fact, for most, this report likely only served to add to their confusion about who

---

6 Christian Smith and Melinda Lundquist Denton, *Soul Searching: The Religious and Spiritual Lives of American Teenagers* (New York: Oxford University Press, 2005).

7 From a *World News Tonight With Peter Jennings* report on January 10, 2005.

God is and what he does. Of course, this is just one little example of the greater sea of confusion kids swim in every day.

- They hear from their favorite celebrities that "spirituality" is very important and that a cuisinart of Judaism and superstition called Kabbalah is a pretty cool dish on the spirituality menu.
- They hear from a certain strain of church leaders that God exists to make us materially prosperous (apparently forgetting that we already live in the most affluent society in the history of the world).
- They hear their parents tell them faith in Christ is a priority, but working hard in school so they can get into the right school so they can get into the right Fortune 500 corner office is a *bigger* priority.
- They hear their pastor say Jesus is the only way—the narrow gate—to eternal life, but then they hear their favorite teachers, the media, and Madison Avenue drill into them the importance of diversity—of many paths to ultimate truth.

In some parts of the Christian world, confusion about God has morphed into apathy and an entirely post-Christian mind-set. Britain, for example, could serve as a warning beacon for us.

Just after World War II, Britain experienced a "religious boom"—it was common for people to attend church every week. Today the percentage of people who attend church weekly in Britain has plummeted to 8 percent, and it's still slipping—in many counties church attendance is on life support at 3 percent. Fewer than 10 percent of British children attend Sunday school. British pollsters are now considering taking the question—"Do you profess a specific faith in Jesus Christ as the risen Lord"—out of their census because it's become a "statistically irrelevant" question. The overwhelming majority of people in the United Kingdom don't have bad opinions of the church—they have no opinion of it because it's simply off their radar screen.

I remember when I was in England several years ago exploring the beginnings of a rebirth of youth ministry in the country. I was invited to sit in on a "religion" class in a London public school. In England the Anglican church is government sponsored, so public schools require kids to attend religion classes. Most are dry and boring. But not always.

Three traditional Anglican churches in Ealing, close to London, pooled their resources to hire 28-year-old Bevan Davis as their "outreach youth minister." That meant Bevan had no responsibility for churched youth—she was free to concentrate on reaching young people in sixth-form public schools (senior highers). So Bevan made school officials an offer that was hard to refuse: In exchange for access to kids at school, she'd plan and lead religion classes for free. On the day that I observed, Bevan and her partner masterfully led kids through a moral decision-making activity that took all but five minutes of the hourlong class. At the end, they connected kids' responses to C. S. Lewis' perspective on morality as a setup to introducing a radical theme—a heart regenerated by faith in Jesus is the only way to address the cancer of amorality in our culture.

Bevan tried to make a pragmatic connection for them by probing what they'd already heard about this through any church connections they had. The kids looked confused and sort of blank, and then one spoke up and said something like: "Um, we don't really know anything about the church or what it believes, actually." These kids didn't have a *bad* opinion of the church; they had *no* opinion of it. From others' comments it was clear that their families had been disconnected from the church for at least two generations.[8]

So how did the Jesus-loving culture that flocked to hear Spurgeon preach morph into the blank stares of those young people? The evidence, collected from the many youth ministry people I spoke to while I was in England, indicates that something had driven a wedge between Jesus and people's everyday experiences. The church lost its "beeline," and in the process lost its relevance in young people's everyday lives. And when that happens it doesn't take long before people simply stop caring about church.

What about here in the United States? On the surface America is still a "Christian nation"—95 percent of Americans say they believe in God, and most pollsters say about 45 percent still attend church every week (some say the actual figure—collected by researchers who literally count heads at weekend worship services—may be more like 17 percent). But remember the top of the faith pyramid—only 10 percent have what NSYR researchers call a "devoted faith." That means all but a "tithe" of American adults and teenagers see a significant connection between their relationship with Jesus and their real-world identity. The growing irrelevance of their faith in Jesus is slowly removing him from kids' everyday reality, making him more like that distant second cousin they met when they were six. They sort of know he's still alive somewhere, and they might send him a Christmas card (if they remember), but they really know nothing about who he is anymore. In their minds he has absolutely no influence on the real events, relationships, and beliefs that propel their lives forward.

We could be, right now, in the same place Britain was in before the church started its slide into single-digit land. Our challenge, therefore, is to make the pursuit of Jesus the central, consuming, desperate focus of our ministry with teenagers. "Remember that second cousin you met when you were a kid?" we ask. "Well, it turns out you're dying from a terminal disease, and only your second cousin's bone marrow can save you now. I've got to introduce you to him again, help you establish a relationship with him, and then humbly ask him to offer what he has to save your life. And oh, by the way, I'm actually quite good friends

---

8 From observations and notes recorded during a three-week trip to Britain, later published in the article "The Case for Post-Christian Youth Ministry," Group Magazine, September/October 2000.

with your second cousin, and I can tell you he's the most interesting, compelling, magnetic person I've ever met—wait 'til you get to know him!"

THE DISTORTED JESUS

I've asked youth pastors all over the country why it's such a challenge to connect teenagers' everyday life experiences to the experience of following Jesus. They most often say it's because the surrounding culture has gone to pot, or kids are so busy with other activities that youth group is way down the list of priorities, or that parents have dropped the ball in teaching the faith at home.

These are all surface explanations that don't get at the core problem—I think the answer to this question is so obvious we've missed it. They simply know little that's true about their "second cousin."

The key is locked up in the quote from N. T. Wright that I included earlier in Chapter 2. Here it is again: "The longer you look at Jesus, the more you will want to serve him. That is of course, if it's the real Jesus you're looking at."[9]

If we're not giving teenagers the real Jesus to look at, or giving them only a tiny peep at that real Jesus, they get a distorted, shallow, undermining sense of who he really is. The Jesus we've unwittingly asked them to follow bears little resemblance to the Jesus who turned the world upside down or the one who promised to "be with us always"—that means, in every aspect of our life.

That's exactly why a "Millennial church" in North Carolina decided to satirize the "fake Jesus" most young people have come to know—to undermine and ridicule their wrong notions of Jesus so they could be reintroduced to him. They took an old-as-bones film about Jesus, extracted four scenes from it, and then recorded their own dialogue to replace the original audio. The result is hilarious (you can check out the videos by going to www.vintage21.com, clicking on the film projector icon, clicking on "Videos," and then clicking on page 2). They gave Jesus a falsetto Mr. Rogers voice, making him the nice Jesus so many kids imagine anyway. Then they cleverly morphed Jesus into a distant rule giver who's out of touch with real life and not at all interested in intimate relationship.

These video parodies are brilliant because they bring into the light the false, ridiculous Jesus that kids often think is the true Jesus. The Vintage21 church made four of these videos as part of a series on the real Jesus—they understood that kids would never trust a fake Jesus with what really matters to them.

Earlier I mentioned my personal deconstruction of the "What Would Jesus Do?" movement—it's pretty much lost its steam now, and I'm secretly thrilled about that. I think a much more unwieldy acronym is nevertheless far more valuable to us right now—it's DWKJWETKWHD. The letters stand for: *Do we know Jesus well enough to know what he'd do?*

---

9 N. T. Wright, *Following Jesus: Biblical Reflections on Discipleship* (Grand Rapids, MI: Eerdmans, 1994), p. ix.

The evidence, soft and hard, says the answer is an unequivocal "no." But there's great hope in embracing this "no" because when we do, we can pursue a ministry strategy similar to the one the Vintage21 church tried with their Jesus-parody videos.

1. First we deconstruct (literally tear apart) the false Jesus that's been imbedded in kids' hearts and minds.
2. Then we reconstruct and reintroduce Jesus to them, and tie everything we do back into the pursuit of him—using Spurgeon's beeline as our gravitational center.

In the next chapter, and in the last two-thirds of this book, I'll take a shot at what it looks like to follow this strategy. But it's important to remember to remember here. The aim of all this—just like the aim of all Bible study, teaching, preaching, and programming in youth ministry—is to spur kids to worship Jesus with "all their heart, soul, mind, and strength, and to love their neighbors as they love themselves." This is how Jesus responded when people asked him to name the most important commandment to follow in life.

The celebrated Christian writer Henri Nouwen served for years as pastor of Daybreak, a Christian community near Toronto for developmentally disabled people that was planted by the L'Arche movement. He wrote this about the co-founder of the L'Arche community in the United States, Father George Strohmeyer—it's a profound expression of what we're aiming for:

This morning I had a chance to speak with him [Father Strohmeyer] about his experience of being a priest for L'Arche.

He told me about his "conversion," the main causes behind his more radical turn to Jesus. As he told his story, it became clear that Jesus was at the center of his life. George has always come to know Jesus with a depth, a richness that few priests have experienced. When he pronounces the name of Jesus you know that he speaks from a deep, intimate encounter. Since his "conversion," his life has become simpler, more hidden, more rooted, more trusting, more open, more evangelical, and more peaceful. For George, being a priest at L'Arche means leading people always closer to Jesus.

I know for sure that there is a long and hard journey ahead of me. It is the journey of leaving everything behind for Jesus' sake. I now know that there is a way of living, praying, being with people, caring, eating, drinking, sleeping, reading, and writing in which Jesus is truly the center. I know this way exists and that I have not fully found it yet.

How do I find it? George gave me the answer: "Be faithful in your adoration." He *did* not say "prayer," or "meditation," or "contemplation." He kept using the word "adoration," worship. This word makes it clear that all my attention must be on Jesus, not on myself. To adore is to be drawn away from my own preoccupations into the presence of Jesus. It means letting go of what I want, desire, or have planned, and fully trusting Jesus and his love.[10]

Can you imagine the joy you'd taste if you could answer "adoration" when others innocently ask you what makes your ministry "successful"? Teenagers caught up in the pursuit and adoration of Jesus will live and breathe and move in the spirit of the first disciples—the same ones who started to believe that if they told a mountain to pick itself up and move, it would.

---

10 From a story by Henri Nouwen in his book *The Road to Daybreak* (Image: Reissue edition, September 1, 1990).

Deconstructing the Trojan Horse

A couple of years ago I wrote a column for Group Magazine titled "The Trojan Horse." In it, I attempted to expose what I think is a false momentum in some of today's Christian music. Most people know that a Trojan horse is a metaphor for an enemy that looks very much like a friend. It's rooted in a story from Homer's *Iliad*, where the Greeks offer their sworn foes, the Trojans, a giant wooden horse, ostensibly as a peace offering. But after the unsuspecting Trojans drag the horse inside their city walls, Greek soldiers drop out of the horse's hollow belly and open the city gates to their army, which rushes through the gates and captures Troy.

"Trojan horse" is still a term we use in our everyday lives. In the computer world, a Trojan horse is a "destructive program that masquerades as a benign application." Often, these programs promise to rid your computer of viruses, but instead they *introduce* viruses. The reason I brand some Christian music with a Trojan horse label is that, while presenting itself as a Jesus-centered alternative to the rotten, profane music of the mainstream culture, it often extols a Jesus who looks a lot like a "divine butler" or a "cosmic therapist."

> "Whatever we're doing to help kids get to know the real Jesus, they're somehow not getting it— actually, they're not getting *him*."

For example, one popular Christian band sings: "Faithful are your ways / I always feel your grace around me / Quickly will I call, quickly will you answer my cry / Carefully will you bring everything I need in my life." I think the Trojan horse belief in this lyric is that Jesus will "quickly" bring me "everything I need in my life."

That sounds great—just what I need, and frankly just what I expect...from my divine butler. Of course God *is* a good and generous father who delights in providing for us, but he's *not* the great vending machine in the sky as the song implies. Put another way, too much of our Christian music—actually, too much of our Christian teaching, curriculum, marketing, T-shirt slogans, and even our conventional ways of praying—implies that God is the person behind the crackly voice coming through the drive-through squawk box. We tell the person behind the box what we want while we scan the happiness menu, and then we drive up to the window and this guy we've never really met (and don't really intend to meet) hands us our bag of happiness.

Maybe that sounds over the top—it would to me, if I hadn't been staring at the results of the *National Study of Youth and Religion* and talking to teenagers and youth pastors about this for the last two years. Whatever we're doing to help kids get to know the real Jesus, they're somehow not getting it—actually, they're not getting *him*. I think there are some big clues as to why this is happening, but it's painful to follow them.

Last week I did an online poll with the thousands of youth leaders who receive our weekly e-newsletter (and by the way, you can subscribe to this helpful e-mail resource at www.youthministry.com). I asked:

How well are your teenagers getting to know Jesus through the ministry of your church? [I] don't mean how well they're learning the Bible or your church's doctrine—[I'd] like to know how often they're specifically focusing on Jesus.

Here's how youth leaders responded:

- Only one out of seven (14.9 percent) answered "very well."
- More than half (51.2 percent) answered "OK" (34.7 percent), "not real well" (14 percent), or "not at all" (2.5 percent).
- The remaining youth leaders (33.9 percent) answered "pretty well."[1]

If youth ministry doesn't exist to help teenagers get to know Jesus "very well," we might as well admit our passions and energy and interests lie elsewhere—we're cup-holder people. It's hard to admit that maybe 85 percent of youth-group teenagers aren't getting to know Jesus intimately at church, but there it is.

And if so few teenagers are getting to know Jesus "very well," it likely means they're in danger of embracing a Jesus who's really a divine butler or a cosmic therapist. That can be more destructive than not introducing him at all. Here's why—the real Jesus doesn't always do what the fake Jesus promises he will. And even more important, it's impossible to have an intimate relationship with a fake Jesus. Once I open my gates to let in Trojan horse Jesus—the nice, obedient, happy-making servant I was promised he'd be—I find he's just not strong enough to build my real life on.

Also, when I get close to Trojan horse Jesus, he isn't all that attractive or interesting. But because I've invited a shallow, deferential, self-serving *idea* of

---

1 From an October 2006 survey of youth leaders subscribing to the YouthMinistry .com e-newsletter.

Jesus into my life, I'm not real motivated to invite the real Jesus inside my gates to kick out his impostor.

And evidence from the *National Study of Youth and Religion* shows that a whole lot of teenagers haven't yet invited the real Jesus inside their gates. Put another way, they have a Trojan horse Jesus sitting in their life's courtyard. Just as the enemy of "great" is "good," the enemy of the true Jesus (to use N. T. Wright's illustration) is the Trojan horse Jesus. And Trojan horse Jesus has infiltrated every aspect of contemporary youth ministry, not just its music.

OUR DIRTY LITTLE BEAUTIFUL SECRET

Just a week ago I was sitting around a table with six youth pastors in the Midwest—they were invited to have lunch with me by a youth ministry professor who's a good friend of mine. He asked these particular men and women to join us because their ministries are widely seen as very effective. We spent two hours talking about Jesus-centered youth ministry.

The deeper we dove into conversation, the more unsettling it became. Finally, one of the youth pastors looked at me with sad-but-determined eyes and said, "I don't think kids walking into our church get to see what it looks like to live as Christians. Most are just there to be with their friends. Our committed Christian kids don't like it—they can't really worship because it's not a worshipful environment. We have attenders, but no community."

Another spoke up, obviously feeling the freedom to finally drag into the light what he'd been too afraid to say. "The word 'Christian' has taken on alternate meanings in today's culture—we need to throw it out," he said. "We need to debunk how [teenagers] have been brought up to see Jesus, and what worship is all about. If we could just shut down for a year…"

The first speaker jumped in and said, "I'd love to shut down for a year! Sometimes we're so comforting and so kind and so welcoming we miss the hard edges of Jesus."

He went on to describe a conversation he'd had with one of his adult leaders after all of the teenagers in that leader's small group quit the group. For more than two years the youth pastor and the adult leader had worked hard to make the small-group environment safe and welcoming. But the kids finally decided they couldn't stand any more talk about Jesus being the "only way" to salvation.

I asked the other youth pastors at the table to respond to what these two guys were talking about. One tried to probe deeper into the small-group story, clearly skeptical that an entire small group of teenagers would quit only because the leader emphasized Jesus too much. He asked the first speaker if maybe he'd given up too quickly on the group or whether he'd worked hard enough to build a warm relational environment in the group. The first speaker responded that the group had been functioning for two years, and the environment was just as warm and relational as their other small groups.

The group sat in uncomfortable silence for a moment.

Then another youth pastor spoke up: "I spent some time this year leading a mission trip overseas—something happened inside of me during that time. When I came back, I told my kids, 'I'm sick of being a Christian—I'm ready to become a Christ follower.' For the kids in my church, there's nothing I've ever said that resonated more with them, or longer. These are kids who've grown up in the church, and they want more."

Clearly, the "let's shut down for a year" comment had stirred something deep in these leaders. By the time lunch was over, three of the six had openly admitted they wished they could destroy the Trojan horse Jesus in their ministry, clearing the way to rebuild on the foundation of the Jesus of Scripture. Effectively, they were longing to fashion a ministry that was far more Jesus-centered.

Now, these were all highly educated, trench-tested veteran youth pastors who'd each been at their churches for many years. They each had hundreds of kids in their ministries. They were clearly mature in their faith and admired for their leadership skills. There was no embittered sense of burnout in them—quite the contrary, actually. I could sense they were all more passionate about youth ministry than ever before—they just didn't like what their ministries had become. And they knew that a few little tweaks or the latest tips and techniques would not get the job done.

Half of them were hungering to know Jesus more deeply and outwardly wishing they could implode their ministry without losing their job.

A GAME PLAN FOR DECONSTRUCTION

This chapter is all about the deconstruction phase of building a Jesus-centered ministry—the pragmatic alternative to "shutting down" your youth ministry for a year to kick the Trojan horse out. I think deconstruction can happen as a central practice in your ministry—the slow dismantling of the Trojan horse followed by dragging its parts to the dump outside your gates. But we'll need to use a pretty big tool from Jesus' toolbox to do it. That tool is called: "Teaching teenagers (and ourselves) to think critically and biblically."

If we don't use critical and biblical thinking to vigorously "push back" against false descriptions of Jesus and the Christian life—and teach kids to do the same—we've abdicated our calling as shepherds (put another way, we let the enemies of God wheel a Trojan horse right into our ministry). Critical thinking and biblical thinking are the "rod and staff" of a shepherd—the staff is for rescuing; the rod is a weapon made for defending against those who would steal or harm the sheep.[2] Teenagers need to be rescued from the subtle lies about Jesus and the Christian life that are ensnaring them, and they need shepherds who will use their "rods" to beat back the creeping Christian-like untruths that are stalking them.

Lazy thinking says, "We hold these truths to be self-evident."

Critical and biblical thinking says, "We uphold no truths as self-evident but those that have been critically pursued and found to be in union with God's Word, both written and living."

2 Description from Light of the Word Ministries, www.lightofword.org.

Critical and biblical thinking asks questions such as

- Is it true from every biblical angle?
- Is it true experientially within the whole body of Christ?
- Is it true in biblical context?
- Is it true within the boundaries of things Jesus actually said and did?
- Is it true based on what I already know is true about Jesus and the kingdom of God?
- Is it true on the face of it?
- Is the foundation or source of the information true, or has it been distorted somehow?
- Is it the full truth, or does it represent only disconnected snippets of truth?
- Is it a culturally bent truth that serves a self-centered agenda?

Let me put this another way. If deconstruction is the first step toward rebuilding a Jesus-centered youth ministry, then we'll need some carefully placed explosives (critical and biblical thinking) to implode the crumbling structure of what we're currently doing.

Ever see a building implode? If not, you'll get an eyeful at www.implosionworld.com. Tom Harris, vice president of content for the great Web site HowStuffWorks.com, says demolition experts implode a building this way:

> The basic idea of explosive demolition is quite simple: If you remove the support structure of a building at a certain point, the section of the building above that point will fall down on the part of the building below that point. If this upper section is heavy enough, it will collide with the lower part with sufficient force to cause significant damage. The explosives are just the trigger for the demolition. It's gravity that brings the building down.
>
> Demolition blasters load explosives on several different levels of the building so that the building structure falls down on itself at multiple points. When everything is planned and executed correctly, the total damage of the explosives and falling building material is sufficient to collapse the structure entirely, so clean-up crews are left with only a pile of rubble.[3]

Harris includes a helpful diagram in his description that pinpoints where the first, second, and third rounds of explosives are set. The first set is placed at the foot of the building's center supports, the second set is placed at the foot of the outer supports, and the third is placed near the tops of both the center and outer supports.

---

3 From the description of implosion at www.howstuffworks.com, written by Tom Harris.

You can see the strategy here—blast the foundational center support first, and then collapse the sides and the top of the building toward that center.

If all this sounds pretty apocalyptic, it's nothing compared to actually watching an implosion. But more and more youth pastors, just like those who met with me for our little round-table lunch in the Midwest, are sensing that implosion—a blowing out of their ministry's central supports, causing a collapse of its structure—is their best hope for the kind of Jesus-centered ministry their souls are longing for. And nothing will cut through those central supports better than critical and biblical thinking.

The primary "central support" we have to blow up is our mental model of Jesus. Psychologists have discovered that, because of the overwhelming information our brains have to organize, we tend to hold on to and defend the established way we see something—even when we get new information that challenges our mental model, we hang on to what we've come to believe is the truth.[4]

A great example of this is Richard Jewell, a central figure in the Centennial Olympic Park bombing at the 1996 Summer Olympics in Atlanta, Georgia.

Jewell was working as a private security guard when he discovered a pipe bomb, alerted the police, and helped to evacuate the area before it went off. In the media he was initially celebrated as a hero. But the FBI later grew suspicious of Jewell and leaked information that pointed to him as a suspect.

Even though he was never charged with a crime, the "cloud of suspicion" around Jewell was entrenched—most of us held to our "mental model" of him that judged him as guilty. Two of the bombing victims filed lawsuits against Jewell. Jay Leno called him the "Una-doofus." And the media turned on him with vicious abandon, solidifying the mental model.

Because of Jewell's close association with the crime, suspicion about him has lingered even though he passed a polygraph test, was formally cleared of suspicion by a U.S. attorney investigating the crime, and the real bomber—radical anti-abortion terrorist Eric Rudolph—admitted to the crime. He will likely never be a "neutral" figure to most people.[5]

This strange mental-model dynamic explains why so few kids—and adults—have an accurate understanding of Jesus. Once their understanding of Jesus and the Christian life is established, they tend to ignore or tune out new information that doesn't fit the model.

C. S. Lewis was a master at using critical and biblical thinking to puncture this tendency to cling to mental models—for example, he wrote that Jesus could *only* be a "liar, lunatic, or Lord"—not the sheep-carrying "nice guy" or "Mr. Rogers" or "dime store prophet" many make him out to be.[6] Choose from these three choices, he said, because critical and biblical thinking wipes out all the others.

---

4 From a description of the "mental model" theory first developed by Kenneth Craik for his book *The Nature of Explanation* (1943), now out of print.

5 From a description of the story of Richard Jewell at www.wikipedia.org.

6 C. S. Lewis, *Mere Christianity* (New York: Macmillan, 1952).

So to destroy the "central support" of a ministry's *idea of Jesus* without shutting down the ministry, we need an array of explosives placed properly:

1. Train teenagers to deconstruct Jesus' words and actions.
The first step in breaking down kids' current mental model of Jesus is to ask three imploding questions, continuously:

- What did Jesus *really* say? (What was the context of his remarks—who was he speaking to, where was he speaking, and why was he speaking?)
- What did Jesus *really* do? (In the context of "normal behavior" in his culture, what impact did his actions have on those who heard him—both positive and negative?)
- How did people *really* experience Jesus? (What is the array of emotional reactions people had to Jesus, and why did they react that way?)

You can train kids to apply these three filtering questions to literally any scripture passage about Jesus. This is really not a hard skill for anyone to learn with a little practice. For example, I'm going to close my eyes right now (really) and stab my finger somewhere in John's gospel. OK, my finger ended up in John 16—in a middle chunk of the chapter titled "Jesus' Death and Resurrection Foretold" (from the NASB). That portion is John 16:16-22. A quick scan of the passage using the three filtering questions yields this harvest:

- *What did Jesus really say?* Well, during the Passover supper before his crucifixion, he warned his disciples—the ones who still thought he had come to lead Israel out of bondage to their Roman oppressors—that he was going away for a little while. When that made them scratch their heads, he bluntly told them they'd soon be consumed with sorrow while others rejoiced and promised that their tears would eventually turn to joy. He compared what they were about to go through to a woman giving birth.
- *What did Jesus really do?* There's so much kindness in Jesus' tone and behavior. He's about to go through one of the most brutal, torturing deaths ever devised by humans, and he's concerned about the depth of hopelessness and sorrow his friends are about to experience because of it. He paints a powerful picture of pain leading to joy, and solemnly promises that they'll see him again.
- *How did people really experience Jesus?* They were confused, worried, and a little panicked.

After you ask the three questions, you ask kids to sum up what new things they've learned because of them. Now, I'm saying we can simply start using these critical filtering questions every time we crack open our Bible to one of the gospels.

The more we do, the more kids will learn to tear apart their false beliefs about Jesus and his kingdom. And they'll be part of the implosion team, not passive observers who watch from a safe distance.

Another high-profile way to accomplish the same deconstructing purpose in your group is to create a permanent fixture in your youth room—a large "Jesus Did/Jesus Didn't" poster. To kick off this ongoing strategy in your group, give kids each a piece of paper that has two columns on it—one column labeled "Jesus Did" and the other "Jesus Didn't."

Choose a chapter from one of the four gospels, and then get kids in small groups to simply read through that chapter looking for things Jesus embraced, advised, or did. They should list those things under the "Jesus Did" column. Then, to get them thinking even more, have them go back through that list and think of the opposites of each thing they've listed.

For example, if they write, "He healed people of sicknesses," on the "Jesus Did" side, they could write, "He didn't charge anyone a fee for healing." After small groups finish this exercise, combine their lists into one list on a large piece of poster board—this is something you can post permanently in your youth room and add to it as time goes on. Whenever you teach or lead a Bible study, stop at least once along the way to ask kids to create a specific Jesus Did/Jesus Didn't list based on the teaching or scripture passage—and then add their findings to your master list posted on a wall.

The key is to train kids to mentally put the brakes on whenever they read or hear anything about Jesus—to push back against "self-evident truths." Get them used to thinking about the true Jesus in everything you do—you'll literally see fruit from this subtle, mental-model underminer the first time you do it.

2. Challenge kids with much, much better questions about Jesus and his kingdom.

Jesus used great questions to teach his followers how to think critically and biblically. My friend Bob Krulish, the director of pastoral staff at my church in Denver, once scoured all four gospels to extract every single question Jesus asked—he ended up with an astonishing 287 questions! And what explosive questions He asked—so potent with critical thinking:

- If a man receives circumcision on the Sabbath that the Law of Moses may not be broken, are you angry with Me because I made an entire man well on the Sabbath? (John 7:23)
- I showed you many good works from the Father; for which of them are you stoning Me? (John 10:32)
- Simon, son of John, do you truly love Me more than these? (John 21:15)
- Which is easier to say to the paralytic, "Your sins are forgiven," or to say, "Get up, take your mat and walk?" (Mark 2:9)
- Which is lawful on the Sabbath: to do good or to do evil, to save life or to kill? (Mark 3:4)

- How can Satan drive out Satan? (Mark 3:23)
- Don't you see that nothing that enters a man from the outside can make him "unclean"? (Mark 7:18)
- Why then is it written that the Son of Man must suffer much and be rejected? (Mark 9:12)
- Salt is good, but if it loses its saltiness, how can you make it salty again? (Mark 9:50)
- Why do you call Me good? (Mark 10:18)
- What then will the owner of the vineyard do? (Mark 12:9)

I could go on and on with this list. Jesus literally peppered his followers and religious leaders with critical-thinking questions, setting explosive after explosive under the central supports propping up their false mental models of God and his kingdom.

We can do likewise. That sounds easy enough, but good critical-thinking questions about Jesus and his kingdom are at a premium in youth ministry today. I learned this truth all over again when a youth ministry near my Group Magazine offices agreed to let us bring our cameras into their small-group ministry for a "ministry makeover." Essentially, they invited us to study their youth ministry, diagnose any problems we found, and offer a "prescription" for change. We decided to confine our focus to the ministry's small-group ministry. We worked with the volunteer leader of the mixed-gender group for high school seniors—his name was Jonny.

When my team gathered to pore over the hours of video we took of Jonny's small group in action, one of the first things we noticed was how bad questions allow Trojan horse Jesus to stay inside the ministry's gates, and how really great critical-thinking questions can invite the real Jesus inside instead.

I noticed that after Jonny asked a discussion question, awkward silence would often follow, or one of his kids would ask him to clarify the question. For example, in a pre-makeover small-group gathering, the topic was "The Role of the Church in Your Life." Jonny asked the group, "We just touched on something that I want you to talk about—what is church supposed to be?" Because the question was too broad and general, the kids had no idea how to answer.

We suggested to Jonny that Jesus gave the best examples of critical-thinking discussion questions, and that his questions were always surprising, specific, and personal. The more surprising, specific, and personal the question, the more likely Jonny would be able to generate deeper (imploding) discussions. We challenged Jonny to make his questions more startling, target only one point with them, and find ways to make them personal.

So for the group's makeover night, Jonny asked his kids: "Which word comes closest to describing the way you see Jesus—nice, fierce, or mysterious? Explain." (This question is from a loopy little resource I created called *JC Q's:*

150 Jesus-Centered Discussion Questions—it's a big, oversized deck of laminated cards held together by a metal ring.) The resulting discussion was lively, intense, and long. Kids were enjoying, really enjoying, thinking about Jesus using the filter of a good critical-thinking question. That night Jonny had trouble *stopping* the discussion when his biggest problem had always been *starting* one. I could just see kids' mental models of Jesus crumbling, right before my eyes.

Most of us don't ask very good questions because we *assume* we already know how to ask the kind of questions kids can't stop talking about. That's the problem Jonny, our makeover youth leader, had—but he didn't know it. The solution to this problem is simply to practice creating and asking good questions until it becomes almost second nature.

Let's play with this right now. I've just extracted a Jesus-centered question from a recent Bible study in Group Magazine: "Why does God instruct believers to regularly remember Jesus' sacrifice on the cross?"

Since I've already considered and "improved" this question before including it in the Bible study, this will be a worthy challenge for me. But before I take a whack at improving this question, it's good to remember, again, that the best critical-thinking discussion questions are always surprising, specific, and personal. Let me tell you what I mean.

- *Surprising* means you include something in the question that would take most people off guard. One way to do that is to take a random object—any little trinket sitting on your desk, for example—and use it as the spark for a surprising question about Jesus.
- *Specific* means you narrow the question from a broad focus to a very narrow focus. Your question should focus on only one well-defined target. So many bad questions are really two questions in one—one question per question, please.
- *Personal* means the question includes something that requires a personal response, not a theoretical response. I mean it requires people to share out of their heart, not just their head.

Now, I'm going to stop here for a moment and see how I can make my test question better reflect Jesus' standards.

(Two minutes later.)

OK, here's what I came up with: "Let's say you open your Bible in the morning and find that God has used his yellow highlighter to mark every place that references Jesus' sacrifice on the cross—why might he do that to your Bible?"

Here's what I did. I grabbed the yellow highlighter sitting right in front of me and then asked God to give me a way to use it to add surprise to the question. Then I remembered to keep the question simple and make it personal.

This kind of quick exercise is something that you can use over and over to improve the quality of your questions about Jesus. It's not hard at all, once you've practiced it a few times. How do I know? We've now trained thousands of youth workers to master it in less than 20 minutes at our youth ministry training events all over the country.

Share this skill with your kids' parents and your adult and student leaders so they can learn to ask better Jesus-centered questions—the more people you have asking better questions, the faster your "central supports" will implode. Do this by challenging them to come up with a Jesus-centered question, and then hand that question to a partner who will make it more surprising, specific, and personal. You can cycle the questions back and forth as many times as you like. They'll come out of this little question-asking boot camp with a radically improved ability to engage kids about Jesus. The idea is to get every leader in your ministry asking great critical-thinking questions about Jesus all the time—to saturate your ministry with them just as Jesus did. Incorporate them into your Bible studies, messages, discussion times, small groups, retreats, conversations...everything.

3. Use humor and satire to expose kids' false mental models of Jesus.

Steve Case is a longtime youth minister and a contributing editor for Group Magazine. He's long used his extensive collection of "Jesus junk"—action figures and posters and night lights—to spark critical thinking in his kids. For example, he recently acquired his "greatest addition" to his collection—a 12-inch hot-pink Jesus figure that works like a Magic 8-Ball. You ask him a question and then turn him over to get an answer such as "Let me ask my father" on the little floating triangle.

Steve uses these junky items to teach his teenagers to see the irony underlying the typically lazy ways we think of Jesus. When teenagers learn to laugh at the ridiculous Jesus, to throw stones at Trojan horse Jesus, they're simultaneously exploding their mental models of him.

This is exactly what the Vintage21 ministry was thinking when they created those satirical and hilarious video spoofs of Jesus using snippets from an old, campy movie about him paired with a new audio track of dialogue. Vintage21 took that idea even further when they created their own eight-episode sitcom called *The Believer Way*. Here's the ministry leaders' explanation for this project:

In the spring of 2004 [we] spent ten weeks in the book of Hebrews. It was clear the recipients of this letter were good-hearted, but a bit confused. You see, while they followed Jesus, they also questioned whether or not there needed to be something else added to the equation: angels, Jewish tradition, the Prophets, and more. This might seem like a foolish mistake, but we're still guilty of it today, with things such as small group Bible studies, "quiet times," and Christian paraphernalia. While all of these things can be valuable, and often help us follow God, we need to be careful not to let them get in the way of what's most important: Jesus Christ. The sincere characters of our satirical sitcom "The Believer Way" struggle to follow God with their hearts, but often end up following tradition and religion instead.[7]

You can buy the entire "season" of *The Believer Way* for just $20 at www.vintage21 .com. I'm impressed with everything about this strategy, though some episodes really hit while others miss. The point is that they're trying to explode the central supports of kids' mental models of Jesus and what it means to follow him.

You can accomplish the same mission on a smaller scale:

- *Challenge teenagers to create contemporary versions of Jesus' parables in the form of mini-dramas that are funny.*

    Think of the possibilities: the parable of the two foundations in Luke 6 (your teenagers could do a takeoff on the popular show *Extreme Makeover: Home Edition*); the parable of the good Samaritan in Luke 10 (they could make the beaten man a homecoming king and the Samaritan could be a fan of Kevin Federline's rap music or the winner of the state spelling bee); or the parable of the wedding feast in Luke 14 (the setting could be the bleachers at a Friday night football game instead of a wedding).

- *Use funny film clips or portions of funny TV shows to get them thinking about the differences between Trojan horse truths and biblical truths.*

    Again, Steve Case uses animated TV shows popular with kids as sparks to exploring Jesus through irony. He says: "My teenagers love the Cartoon Network and Fox's *Simpsons* and *Family Guy*. Most of them can quote Stewie or Hank Hill at the drop of a hat. And all of the great Warner Brothers Classic cartoons are now available on DVD. We use this stuff to get kids laughing then get them thinking. For example...in many episodes of *King of the Hill* Hank and his family must deal with problems at church (the one where Bobby joins the church youth group will make you blow coffee out your nose)."

- *Take your teenagers to a performance by a Christian stand-up comedian, or watch one on DVD.*

If you've ever been to a national youth ministry convention, one staple on the main stage is always a Christian comedian or comedy team. It looks like entertainment but it's more like ministry, because nothing is more powerful than comedy at forcing us to look at common things differently. For ideas, go to www.christiancomedyindex.com, which bills itself as the "ultimate listing of Christian comedians."

The point is that we can explode the central supports of a false mental model of Jesus when we use humor as a portal into critical and biblical thinking. And few things are more exciting to watch than an old, tired building imploding.

---

7 Taken from www.vintage21.com.

Once you clear the rubble, you'll be ready for the grand adventure of your life—building a "beeline" life and a "beeline" ministry. I mean, what would your life look like, and your youth ministry, if literally everything you did was connected by a beeline back to Jesus?

The rest of this book is simply a playful, creative exploration of what the beeline might look like (and does look like) in the 10 primary pursuits of youth ministry. I've tackled the 10 in no particular order, though some chapters fit with each other better than others. To kick off each of these chapters I've asked some of the sharpest people in youth ministry to take a stab at the beeline—as a kick-start into each pursuit.

In the introduction to this book I said I didn't want to depend solely on the sonar of my own voice—that's why there are so many voices represented. By the last page, I think our collective "sonar" will map out a shape that looks a lot like a cross.

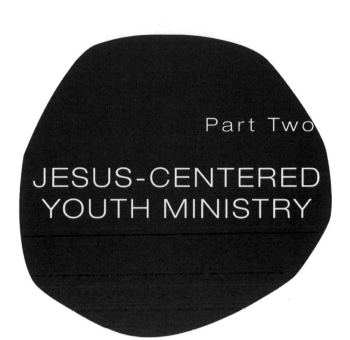

Part Two

JESUS-CENTERED YOUTH MINISTRY

Discipleship

(WITH AN INTRODUCTION BY DUFFY ROBBINS)

PROTECTING OUR KIDS FROM JESUS

I'd been scheduled to speak at a large regional denominational event out West, and about two weeks before the event I received a phone call from a woman on the "design team" who wanted to review with me some basic details of the conference schedule and travel plans. All in all, it was pretty routine.

That's when she added, without any hint of irony, this additional word of direction:

"Please, when you give your talks to the kids, we've decided as a design team to ask that you not mention the name of Jesus. We don't mind if you talk about God; in fact, we hope you will. But we hope you'll understand that talking about Jesus will offend some of our young people, and we don't want to do anything that will make them feel uncomfortable..."

I tried to imagine a doctor who refused to tell her patient of his disease because it might, after all, trouble him. Or the spelling teacher who didn't have the heart to tell his students that they were consistently misspelling certain words because he didn't want to discourage them. Or the traffic cop who couldn't bring himself to ask the driver to please keep his truck off of the sidewalk because he didn't want the driver to think he was unfriendly.

In my mind's eye I saw the furrowed brows of the design team members as they wrestled with "the Jesus problem."

A NEW KIND OF MODESTY

Today, modesty seems as out of date as Pong and penny loafers—no topic is taboo, no indignation untelevised, no truth held back. That's why it's striking that we in the church have finally found a modesty that we can feel good about: We can be modest about Jesus.

Now, please understand, I'm entirely sympathetic with the motives that must have led these good folks to "design" the Designer out of their youth event. After all, they wanted to make the conference a safe place for kids to ask questions and feel accepted and comfortable. I agree with that. That's important. But just because we want all patients—no matter how sick—to feel welcomed into the hospital, that doesn't mean that we warmly accept every sickness and germ. And it certainly doesn't mean that we hold back on the cure because we're afraid of offending the virus. This is when a "generous orthodoxy" becomes a "disingenuous orthodoxy."

Several years ago I heard that the archbishop of Canterbury said the Church of England was "dying of good taste." I hope it's not in poor taste to say so, but I fear the same may be happening to us in youth ministry.

AFRAID OF JESUS

In Matthew 14:22-33 Peter and his shipmates were frightened by a storm that railed against them on one awful night—it was a fury of horizontal rain, howling wind, and smothering darkness. But as scary as that storm must have been, that wasn't what really got them screaming and gasping. After all, some of those on the boat were fishermen by trade. They'd seen storms before. And they were making their way across the Sea of Galilee with the kind of deliberation we might expect from professional watermen.

No. What really shook everybody up that night in the midst of the stormy turmoil was when Jesus arrived on the scene (14:26). Now this was no longer the story of valiant sea-crossing in the midst of a storm; it was the story of the Son of God quieting the wind and the waves with a rebuke. And that changes everything. The big issue is no longer about *working harder* while being very careful that *nobody rocks the boat*. Now the issue is obedience to the One who is the Son of God.

I think a lot of us in youth ministry have come to terms with the scary parts of our work: unruly kids, unhappy parents, bad food, lock-ins, church vehicles, the church board. Sure, it's a storm, but we know these waters. What makes some of us uneasy is when Jesus shows up.

One of the great temptations in youth ministry is to keep our kids safe. "OK, sure, it's a storm out there, but let's just keep rowing and we'll get them across to the other side." So we concentrate on nice little programs—stuff that's affirming and won't offend anybody. We try not to talk too much about sin. We avoid God's harder edges. And for pity's sake, let's go low-key when we talk about Jesus.

It reminds me of one of the great scenes in C. S. Lewis' *The Lion, the Witch, and the Wardrobe*, when the children first hear about Aslan, the mysterious, frightening, Christ figure who's rumored to be on the prowl.

> "Is—is he a man?" asked Lucy.
> "Aslan a man!" said Mr. Beaver sternly. "Certainly not.
> I tell you he is the King of the wood and the son of the great Emperor-Beyond-the-Sea. Don't you know who is the King of Beasts? Aslan is a lion—the Lion, the great Lion."
> "Ooh!" said Susan, "I'd thought he was a man. Is he—quite safe? I shall feel rather nervous about meeting a lion."
> "That you will, dearie, and no mistake," said Mrs. Beaver, "if there's anyone who can appear before Aslan without their knees knocking, they're either braver than most or else just silly."

"Then he isn't safe?" said Lucy.

"Safe?" said Mr. Beaver. "Don't you hear what Mrs. Beaver tells you? Who said anything about safe? 'Course he isn't safe. But he's good. He's the King, I tell you."[1]

KEEPING OUR KIDS SAFE FROM JESUS

I never agreed in that phone call to refrain from talking about Jesus. I couldn't. First of all, that's not me. And second, that's not the gospel. I *did* do the event, and I *did* talk about Jesus (a little more than normal). And what we all experienced that weekend, once again, was Jesus Christ meeting the desperate yearnings of kids restless and helpless in their adolescent storms.

He's *not* safe, but, oh he is so good.

—DUFFY ROBBINS
Professor of Youth Ministry, Eastern University

Duffy Robbins closes his introduction to this chapter with my favorite scene from the Narnia books—C. S. Lewis makes such a profound theological and practical statement about Jesus in the midst of this narrative. And that's where the film version of *The Lion, the Witch, and the Wardrobe* stumbles. In the book Lewis creates a vivid image of Aslan/Christ that charges the atmosphere in the Beavers' home. We're magnetically drawn to him at the very time we feel something like dread. Lewis could pull this off because his relationship with Jesus was intimate. But the film version of Aslan leaves me cold— I'm neither drawn to him nor frightened by him. In all the hubbub surrounding the release of the 2005 film, its director, Andrew Adamson, went out of his way to make sure potential filmgoers knew he hadn't made a "Christian" film. He made no claims to an intimate relationship with Jesus. And I think that's exactly why Lewis' dead-on metaphor for Christ didn't translate to film—Adamson was too distant from him to breathe Jesus' essence into Aslan.[2]

I think Adamson's portrayal of Aslan mirrors the typical ways we portray Jesus in the church—we're often so distant from who he actually was and what he actually did that we convey a Jesus who's indistinct, dull, and..."tame." Among my other disappointments with the WWJD movement, I think its worthy goal of helping us imagine what Jesus might do if he were faced with the decisions and challenges of our everyday lives actually distanced the real Jesus from many. Our answer to

---

1 C. S. Lewis, *The Lion, the Witch, and the Wardrobe* (New York: MacMillan, 1950, pp. 74–76.

2 From an interview with Andrew Adamson conducted on November 19, 2005, and published on www.gospelcom.net.

WWJD is based on our current understanding of him, and that's the fatal flaw in the WWJD software program that made it crash. Here's what I mean.

I've already said that DWKJWETKWHD (*Do we know Jesus well enough to know what he'd do?*) is a much more useful acronym than WWJD. An even more useful acronym (after this book I'm thinking of writing another book titled *The Bonfire of the Acronyms*) is WDJD—it stands for "What did Jesus do?" I think it's far more important to understand what Jesus *actually did* than ponder what He *might do* if he were in our shoes. WDJD draws us into a charged intimacy with Jesus; WWJD can force us into a mental exercise that makes us distant observers of him, not relaters with him.

In that light, it's crucial to think about what Jesus actually *did* when he set about making disciples out of the guys he rescued from the Island of Misfit Toys. Here's my simple WDJD breakdown:

1. *He revealed God by making His own intimate relationship with the Father the first priority and then invited others into that relationship.*
2. *He revealed God by teaching the truth about him.*
3. *He revealed God by forcing his disciples to depend on him.*

These three WDJD truths will serve as our road map through the rest of this chapter. Even though I'm a guy, I still love a good road map. So let's get going.

JESUS LIVED INTIMATELY WITH GOD AND INVITED OTHERS INTO THAT INTIMACY

When Tom Melton, my friend and the senior pastor at my church, describes the character and personality of Jesus, he often has to collect himself and wipe away the tears that come so quickly. I'm riveted by those tears—they preach louder than his words. I know he loves Jesus and is captured by him. I know he's experienced intimacy in his relationship with Jesus. And as I watch the tears roll down his cheeks, I'm drawn to Jesus.

That's exactly the impact teenagers are longing for—they want to be invited into our intimate relationship with Jesus. In a survey we gave to more than 10,000 Christian kids, three-quarters of them said they want a youth leader "whose personality and lifestyle makes me want to learn more about Jesus."[3]

Now, of course, there's an uncomfortable question lurking here: Does my intimacy with Jesus invite the people around me to hunger to know him better? If it does, it's only a burning reflection of his beauty. I find it magnetic, humbling, and profound that Jesus spent so much time retreating from the crowds, his friends, his family—everyone—to spend intimate time with his Father. "But Jesus often withdrew to lonely places and prayed" (Luke 5:16). Jesus often proclaimed that he was "one" with his Father—how did he know? Well, because he'd spent an

---

3 From a Group Magazine survey of more than 10,000 Christian teenagers attending a Group Workcamp during the summer of 2005, results published in the article "What Kids Really Want," January/February 2006 Group Magazine.

eternity talking with and laughing with and strategizing with and enjoying his Father—alone.

When kids are drawn to Jesus because of something about us, I think they smell the fumes from our intimate encounters with him. Trouble is, life itself works against intimacy. How many truly intimate married couples do you know? Of those you do, I'd bet the million dollars I don't have that they went to war, many times over, to fight for their intimacy.

I love this Bruce Cockburn lyric from his song "Lovers in a Dangerous Time":

When you're lovers in a dangerous time
Sometimes you're made to feel as if your love's a crime—
But nothing worth having comes without some kind of fight—
Got to kick at the darkness 'til it bleeds daylight[4]

Intimacy is a prize that will cost you everything to claim. Life's currents are propelling us down a shallow river of relationships toward the cliffs of loneliness. I know that sounds ridiculously sentimental, but I also know from experience it's true.

This summer God performed a "celebrity smack-down" on me (he was the celebrity; I was the smack-ee). My overlapping responsibilities as editor of Group and creator of the Group Magazine Live conference series, combined with some chronic health problems in my family, had sucked the life out of me. My tank was empty—I knew it, but like a disbelieving driver who is sure there's a gas station just over the next hill, I kept rocking back and forth in the driver's seat, nudging myself a little farther.

That's when God vaulted off the ring stanchions and did a flying belly-flop on me.

It was a Saturday morning. My wife was sick in bed and my two little girls were anxiously pleading for me to get my act together so we wouldn't be late for a family birthday party. They were already strapped into the car waiting in the garage. I was angry. Angry that everything was on my shoulders...again. Angry that my wife was sick—but she couldn't help that, I told myself. Angry at my kids for wanting to be at their birthday party on time—but they couldn't help that, I told myself. So ultimately I was angry at myself, for having an empty tank when I was trying to merge onto my Saturday highway.

In my angry, impatient rush I hurried through the door into our garage but missed that last step. I did one of those 90-degree ankle-buckling falls with a hot latte in one hand and my laptop slung over my other shoulder. It hurt. It really, really, really hurt—so badly that I just let that scream rip from my lungs—the loudest bellow of my life. I pounded the concrete garage floor, and let the dam

---

4 From "Lovers in a Dangerous Time," written and recorded by Bruce Cockburn on the album *Stealing Fire* (1984).

burst that was holding back all my pain, frustration, and anger. Inside the car, my kids watched all of it wide-eyed, like raccoons caught in the flashlight's glare. The garage functioned like an amplifier, making my screams even louder. That's when the neighbors showed up—the new neighbors that I hadn't even met yet. They'd heard my screams and rushed over to see me pounding the floor in a pool of latte.

"What happened?" they cried.

Right about then my disheveled wife rushed into the garage in her robe and asked the same question. Then she looked up and saw our new neighbors standing there. "Hi, I'm Bev," she said, pulling her robe a little tighter around her. Through my clenched teeth I spit out an inaudible indictment—"What a perfect way for the new neighbors to meet us."

Well, it turns out our neighbors are parents of teenagers and thus well practiced at entering into a crisis. They quickly discovered our girls were supposed to be at a birthday party and offered to take them to the party so they wouldn't miss it. My wife gave them directions while I dragged myself into the house and hobbled to a chair so I could elevate my grapefruit ankle. My wife, who'd stayed away from me that morning because of my aforementioned grouchy behavior, got some ice for my ankle, cautiously gave me a tender-ish squeeze, and left me alone.

In the silence I ran back through all of the things that had gone wrong that morning, like a prosecutor laying out the charges before the defendant. In the dock that morning was God. In the middle of my dissertation, God opened his mouth and softly said to me: "Rick, I pull the trigger."

He didn't have to say it twice—I knew exactly what he meant. His love is fierce and passionate and unafraid to stop me in my tracks before I do any further damage. I'm not saying he tripped me on those garage stairs, but I am saying he put me in the adult version of timeout. And in the silence, my tears came. And through the tears I felt him speaking to me again: "Come away with me, Rick."

And so I did. I remembered a mountain monastery I'd visited 20 years ago, when I was just out of college. They had private accommodations for personal retreats, and it was a Trappist monastery, so the monks "kept the silence" for most of the day. I e-mailed them to see if I could reserve one of their little stone "hermitages"—a private cottage with a little kitchen, a bathroom, and a bed. The "guest master" at the monastery told me they were booked up for months, except for two nights during the only week I could get away.

So I packed up a few clothes, a couple of books, my Bible, and a cooler with food and drove three hours to the monastery. I spent the next three days in virtual silence sitting at Jesus' feet—just like Mary in that Mary-and-Martha story. But in my case Jesus was like a fire hydrant. It had been so long since I'd given him more than an hour or so to tell me what was on his mind that he had a lot to say. It was rich, oh-so-rich. I found myself again in his goodness, in his surprising, wild, attractive presence. I came away to the quiet with him, like a midlife couple on a second honeymoon. I can still smell the stillness...the fragrance of his presence and the sweet sound of his voice.

When I returned from the monastery, I told my friend Bob Krulish—director of the pastoral staff at my church—all about my smack-down. Later that day he sent me this note:

> Rick, I know Thursdays are not good days for you, but I go down to the Mount St. Francis retreat center north of Colorado Springs each month for "a day with the Lord." Usually some elders and staff go as well, and I would love to have you join us. If you can't come with us, I sure would encourage you to put it on your schedule—at a time that would fit you. You are wired to hear from the Lord, and stopping everything for a day would catapult you in terms of intimacy. Just a thought and offer!

Wow, reading this note again reminds me all over why I love Bob so much and why he's had such a profound impact on my life. It's a perfect melding of respect, invitation, and admonishment. He's challenging me to get past my attachment to the "small story" of my life and, in faith, invest in the "bigger story" of my life. It makes so much simple sense that "going away to lonely places" to pay attention to God would "catapult you in terms of intimacy," cleaning up your "mirror" a little more so teenagers can see Jesus reflected in you.

Now, your "lonely place" doesn't have to be a monastery (but it could) or a retreat center (but it could)—but it does have to be a *place* that's *lonely*. I mean, we're fooling ourselves if we think our intimacy with God is deepened by shouting at each other over the din of everyday life—like two side-by-side motorcyclists on the freeway. Jesus went *away* to lonely places—and *away* meant someplace outside the sphere of his demanding public responsibilities. Your lonely place could be your garage or your basement or your son's treehouse—as long as it's a place you can guarantee a large chunk of uninterrupted time. And when Scripture records that Jesus "often" went away to lonely places, it's emphasizing that this was a normal, rhythmic part of his life. Listen, no one who ever lived had more reason to maximize his time—think of the number of people *not healed* or *not freed* from demons or *not drawn* into the kingdom of God because Jesus so often left them to be alone with his Father. To be mentored by Jesus is to pay attention to his habits—and going to lonely places was one of his primary habits.

A couple of years ago I started out a training time with some national youth ministry leaders by asking them to get with a partner, and then I gave each pair a brown bag with the same hidden object inside. I gave one person in each pair, the Teacher, permission to reach into the bag and touch the object for just 30 seconds. Then the Teacher had to describe it to his or her partner, the Learner. I told the Teachers they couldn't use the object's name to describe it.

Afterward, I asked the Learners, "What is the object?" Few guessed correctly. Then I asked the Teachers, "What is the object?" Some knew what it was but couldn't describe it well enough for their partner to guess it. Others had no idea what the object was, even after handling it in the bag for 30 seconds.

Then I asked them to pull the object out of their bags—it was a little Gumby-like bendable man. After the laughter died down, I said, "Let's say our little bendy guy represents Jesus. How were the challenges in this activity like the challenges we face in teaching today's kids about Jesus?"

Well, there was some uncomfortable silence. Then one guy spoke up and said something like: "The biggest challenge is knowing Jesus intimately enough to describe him to others—and we've got a lot going on that's keeping us from knowing him intimately." Amen.

One of the Midwest youth pastors I met with for lunch last week said this: "Everything's birthed out of listening. You're growing, so you pass what's happening in you on to the kids in the ministry. [Listening] creates quiet in your heart, and in the quiet everything points back to Jesus."

That leader's comments mesh well with what researchers with the *Exemplary Youth Ministries* study heard when they interviewed pastors, youth pastors, volunteers, and teenagers at each of the 21 chosen churches—they found a shared "come to the quiet" passion running through the leaders. For example, the Rev. Dave Byrum, senior pastor at First United Methodist Church in Valparaiso, Indiana, says: "We put prayer and spiritual formation first with youth. I don't think the cultural expectations of ping-pong and a good time are as necessary as the culture thinks it is. We acknowledge that kids are deeply spiritual people and want to be. They're hungry…We still have fun and play wacky games and ping-pong and share lots of food, but they're more of a by-product than the centerpiece." And an adult volunteer at New Colony Baptist Church in Billerica, Massachusetts, says: "It's Jesus. In all honesty that's the way I see it. We all spend time in prayer—if we didn't, I don't know what would be going on."

The message here is we can more powerfully disciple teenagers when we do what Jesus did and "come away to lonely places." I can't really "afford" to take an entire day away every month to waste time with God—it's a lavish extravagance that my deadlines, my co-workers, my wife, my girls, and my friends pay for. But I'm like a toddler at church who feels so proud when he puts a dollar bill into the offering plate—the only reason I have a dollar to give is because my dad gave it to me.

We'll have no "good treasure" to give teenagers unless we get it from the source of all treasures in our intimate "lonely place" encounters with him. And we offer them these treasures when we carry our intimate encounters with Jesus into our conversations, our teaching, and our actions.

U2's Bono, of all people, is a great role model for me in this. I know that sounds wacky and oddly like hero worship, but I think Bono has managed to consistently drag his intimate relationship with Jesus into the blinding lights of a celebrity-glutted culture. Under the great duress of fame and fortune, he's managed to find repeated ways to let his central-support passion for Jesus spill into all his nooks and crannies.

Last year I read Jann Wenner's Rolling Stone cover interview with Bono[5] and then watched Ed Bradley interview him on *60 Minutes*.[6] When Bradley asked Bono how he's been so successful convincing American leaders to support AIDS research and relief for the African continent, he expected a political/rock star answer. Instead, Bono pointed to his relationship with Jesus.

> Bradley: Is there a secret to your success—the way you've been able to do this?
>
> Bono: It was probably that it would be really wrong beating a sort of left-wing drum, taking the usual bleeding-heart-liberal line.
>
> Bradley (voiceover): Instead he enlisted the ruling right of American politics.
>
> Bono: Particularly conservative Christians, I was very angry that they were not involved more in the AIDS emergency. I was saying, "This is the leprosy that we read about in the New Testament. You know, Christ hung out with the lepers, but you're ignoring the AIDS emergency. How can you?" And, you know, they said, "Well, you're right, actually. We have been. And we're sorry. We'll get involved." And they did.

To Bradley, the story here is how savvy Bono was in co-opting "the ruling right of American politics." He completely missed the meaning behind his "How can you?" What drives Bono's passion for the poor and sick of Africa? Jesus cares about them. And Jesus is everything to Bono, as evidenced in this exchange between Bono and Michka Assayas, author of *Bono: In Conversation With Michka Assayas*:[7]

> Bono: I really believe we've moved out of the realm of karma into one of grace.
>
> Assayas: Well, that doesn't make it clearer for me.
>
> Bono: At the center of all religions is the idea of karma. You know, what you put out comes back to you: an eye for an eye, a tooth for a tooth, or in physics—in physical laws—every action is met by an equal or an

---

5 Jann Wenner, publisher of Rolling Stone magazine, interviewed U2's lead singer Bono for the cover article of the October 2005 issue.

6 Ed Bradley of *60 Minutes* interviewed Bono for a story first aired on the November 20, 2005 show.

7 This conversation is taken from *Bono: In Conversation With Michka Assayas* by Michka Assayas (New York: Riverhead, 2005).

opposite one...And yet, along comes this idea called grace to upend all that "as you reap, so you will sow" stuff. Grace defies reason and logic. Love interrupts...the consequences of your actions, which in my case is very good news indeed, because I've done a lot of stupid stuff.

Assayas: I'd be interested to hear that.

Bono: That's between me and God. But I'd be in big trouble if karma was going to finally be my judge...It doesn't excuse my mistakes, but I'm holding out for grace. I'm holding out that Jesus took my sins onto the Cross, because I know who I am, and I hope I don't have to depend on my own religiosity.

I think this is exactly what it means to invite others into your intimacy with Jesus. In response to Wenner's questions about the role of "religion" in his life, Bono said, "The music that really turns me on is either running toward God or away from God. Both recognize the pivot, that God is at the center of the jaunt."

The more teenagers understand that Jesus is *our pivot*—that our life with him is so real and intimate that it spills over into every conversation and every activity and every counseling session and every laughter-filled outing and every late-night phone call—the more they'll be magnetically drawn to the Jesus you and I are so obviously captivated by.

Now, what are some practical "bridges" or "opportunities to play" that connect into sharing out of our intimacy with Jesus? Here are four ideas:

1. Ask yourself: "Realistically, how desperate am I for God right now?"
If you say "very," skip to number 2.

If you say "honestly, not very," then let's loop back to something I said in Chapter 1—"Our biggest faith battle is remembering to remember God." If you're not consciously desperate for God right now, then you have a rich opportunity to remember him, right now, without the "leverage" of desperation. You can simply choose to remember him by stepping toward something lavish and totally uncalled for—by "coming away" with Jesus for a day, every month. If you think you might just want to do that, you're ready for number 2.

2. If you're ready to set apart one (or even two) days a month to "get away to a lonely place" with Jesus, here are three ways to do it.
(By the way, the idea here is to have absolutely no contact or conversation with others during the course of your day away—that's like inviting your neighbors to join you for the special anniversary dinner you planned to have with your spouse.)

- Ask your senior pastor or other church staffers and adult leaders for suggestions about retreat centers or even private homes where you can spend a day away. You want a place that's comfortable, but has few distractions.

- Most Catholic churches are hard-wired to offer private, secluded places for reflection and pursuing God. Call the Catholic church in your town and ask if such a place exists nearby.
- Go online to find a retreat center near your location. Here a few sites that may lead you to the Promised Land:

  —Retreats Online—www.retreatsonline.com Click on the map, and then on your state, to find retreat centers near you.

  —International Worship & Arts Center—www.worship-arts-network.com /OCretreatcenters.html Click on your region or try the "Links" link.

  —Church 2000—www.church2000.org/Links/conference/info.asp Just plug your state or city or town into the search box.

  —WebRJDesign—www.rjdwebdesign.com/singles/Facilities.asp Click on the CCI/USA link under "Christian Retreats and Conference Centers, Camps and Facilities."

3. Look for "come away with me" moments in the bustle of your everyday life.

In every good marriage there are three kinds of connections—the everyday "on the fly" ways we relate, the "lunch break" ways we relate (we like to call these "quiet times"), and the "come away with me" ways we relate. All are important. But I want to make sure I don't leave a "devaluing" impression about the everyday, every-moment ways we relate with God. In fact, it's this connection that has driven my intimate relationship with God into my own "public square."

My "on the fly" relationship with God is fueled by two things:

- *Talking with God about everything, not just some things.* I call this the "parking space prayer principle." You know how we look down on praying for parking spaces as a trivial, self-centered way of "using" God? I think just the opposite— God is at least as passionately interested in the details of my life as my wife is, so if my focus is riveted on getting a good parking space for some reason, why wouldn't I talk to God about that?
- *Seeing life through the lens of parable.* I'll go into greater depth with this in Chapter 14, "Communication." But the essential practice is to live awake, with a mind-set that assumes God is planting parables all around me, all the time. No matter what the experience, God is speaking through it somehow. He'll speak to me through them if I'll just pay attention.

For example, I'm writing this at home right now, and my wife just let out a shriek because the chili she's cooking for friends tonight burned a little on the bottom. I ran out to the kitchen to see what happened and found her disgusted with herself for not remembering to stir the pot. So right now I pause to ask God what parable he might be telling through this experience. Here it is: "Sin burns my soul, and if I ignore it and leave it on the 'burner' long enough, that burned taste will infiltrate the whole pot." Fortunately for us, and our guests tonight, my wife pulled that pot off as soon as she got a whiff of that burning smell. We were able to salvage the rest of the chili. "Keep short accounts with me." That's what God is trying to tell me. So I stop and thank him for that.

4. Embrace the Bono within.

Here's what I mean. Create a tunnel between your intimate times with God—whether on the fly or not—so what he's pouring into you goes *through you* rather than stops with you. This is about verbalizing whatever God is doing in you today. In my case, this transition was as simple as turning on a spigot—I just decided to drag into the light the conversations, insights, and learnings that pepper my everyday relationship with God. I assume (or trick my brain into thinking) that what happens in my relationship with God is as conversational as what happens in my relationship with my wife, so I talk about him just as naturally. This is especially countercultural in your casual conversations and in those connections you have with non-Christians. So I don't just talk about my wife burning the chili—I talk about what God showed me through the burnt chili. Naturally.

JESUS REVEALED GOD BY TEACHING THE TRUTH ABOUT HIM

In an interview I did with Dr. Christian Smith, I asked him to pinpoint something we should pay attention to in the *National Study of Youth and Religion*. Here's what he said:

> Even though most teens are very positive about religion and say it's a good thing, the vast majority are incredibly inarticulate about religion. They could not explain what they believed—hardly at all. They had extreme difficulty in explaining how it affected their lives, other than to say it makes them happy, helps them have a better day, and helps them make some good moral decisions. It seems like religion operates in the background—it's just part of the wallpaper, part of the furniture. That's important for a couple different reasons. It doesn't seem to us that many teens are being very well-educated in their faith traditions. They aren't being taught how to think and talk about what they believe and how it affects their lives. This is probably the same with parents.[8]

This is exactly how teaching fits into discipleship. And Jesus-centered teaching aims to bring Jesus into the foreground for kids and give them a new ability to articulate why they're following him.

This summer my wife and I created a 12-week class at our church called "The Pursuit of Jesus"—it was open to everyone in the church. Here's how we advertised the class in the bulletin: "A new class just for the summer. No tips and techniques.

---

8 Dr. Christian Smith quoted in the article "The National Study of Youth and Religion: Why Today's Kids Just Don't Get It" in the January/February 2005 issue of Group Magazine.

No life application. No homework. No acronyms. Just Jesus." Our idea was to pursue Jesus for his own sake, not with the church's unrelenting agenda to see everything through a what's-in-it-for-me lens. What if we shoved our running shoes into the starting blocks and then ran as hard as we could after Jesus in the hope of catching him?

Well, we did it. We had people of all ages show up for the class. We discovered they all had one thing in common—they wanted more than what a traditional tips-and-techniques Sunday school class offered. They wanted more of Jesus. No, that's not right. *They needed more of Jesus.* I have to say, it was one of the greatest Jesus adventures of my life. When you're unconcerned about extracting life lessons from Jesus and you explore his nooks and crannies only because you're fascinated and drawn to him, you find yourself worshipping him almost all the time.

Our guiding question for the summer was, "Who do you say Jesus is?" I described the context for this question (Luke 9) in the Introduction.

I'm probably being way too dramatic here, but I believe "Who do you say that Jesus is?" is the *only question* we really need for discipling teenagers. It's such a rich, lifelong, elusive, and satisfying question—I think I'll be pursuing its answer until my last breath.

Because this question—and the pursuit of its answer—is so foundational to teaching the truth about Jesus, I thought it might be helpful if I gave you the 12 topics—snapshots of Jesus, really—that formed the skeleton of our "summer of love." It's a great template for teaching that reveals God the way Jesus did—even though it'll be easy for you to spot ways to improve it. Every class was highly interactive and experiential—we used creative experiences, surprising discussion questions, film, objects, music, art, and worship practices as the means to our lofty end. For each snapshot, I'll give you a little taste of our beeline.

1. Introduction: "Who Do You Say I Am?"

This is the best and primary question of our lives. We used this story about Thomas and Philip and Jesus from John 14:4-9 as the focal point: Jesus said to his disciples: "You know the way to the place where I am going. Thomas said to him, 'Lord, we don't know where you are going, so how can we know the way?' Jesus answered, 'I am the way and the truth and the life. No one comes to the Father except through me. If you really knew me, you would know my Father as well. From now on, you do know him and have seen him.' Philip said, 'Lord, show us the Father and that will be enough for us.' Jesus answered: 'Don't you know me, Philip, even after I have been among you such a long time? Anyone who has seen me has seen the Father.' "

We closed the class by exploring the profound meaning underlying a "progression" my friend Ned Erickson once shared with me: "Get to know Jesus well, because the more you know him, the more you'll love him, and the more you love him, the more you'll want to follow him, and the more you follow him, the more you'll become like him, and the more you become like him, the more you become yourself."9

2. Only Jesus Is Good (Part 1)

We used Jesus' fascinating first response to the rich young ruler—"Why do you call me good?"—as the basis for two classes. Why two? Well, I think Jesus' goodness—expressed in such divergent ways as his preoccupation with healing people and casting out their demons, to his tenderness for the broken and forgotten, to his ferocity directed toward the religious leaders of his day—is really the central aspect of his nature that we just don't "get." We asked people to quickly list things they think are good about Jesus and then defend their list to others. Then we selected a wide array of stories about Jesus that displayed his goodness and asked people to work with a partner to discover and list as many "good things" about Jesus as they could. Then we asked them to condense their lists into a "Jesus definition" of "good."

3. Only Jesus Is Good (Part 2)

Continuing the theme, we set up a simple "taste test" using two different steak sauces to plunge participants into Psalm 34:8—"Taste and see that the Lord is good." How can we experience his goodness if we don't taste him? So we had people list all the tastes they could discern in each of the steak sauces and then had a friend who's a chef reveal his list. It was, um, a lot longer than our lists. Then we asked the chef to tell us how great cooks develop a powerful palate and compared those lessons to what it looks like to taste deeply of Jesus. Then we explored how Jesus defined, and redefined, goodness.

4. Jesus and His Parables

We asked people to tell each other vivid stories from their past. Then we introduced the idea that all of Jesus' parables were crafted to answer two questions: "Who is God?" and "What is life like in God's kingdom?" Jesus knew he had to find a creative way to reveal the personality of his Father and the nature of life in God's kingdom—to translate these great truths into something we could understand. Then we launched them on an adventure to find answers to the two questions by exploring several of Jesus' parables.

5. Jesus and Desperate People

It was cheeky, but we subtitled this one "the 'desperate housewives' He loved." That's because there's a lot to learn from the ragged, fringe people who were drawn to Jesus, and vice versa. And many of the most riveting stories of desperation involved women. We watched a scene from It's a Wonderful Life and explored together the dynamics of desperation.

---

9 Ned Erickson learned this progression from his ministry partners in Young Life.

6. Jesus and True Family

This was perhaps the most challenging class of the series. When we examined what Jesus really had to say about family, we discovered he wasn't as family-friendly as we'd all been led to believe. Among many other passages, we focused on Matthew 10:34-39: "Do not suppose that I have come to bring peace to the earth. I did not come to bring peace, but a sword. For I have come to turn 'a man against his father, a daughter against her mother, a daughter-in-law against her mother-in-law—a man's enemies will be the members of his own household." Because Jesus said his Father had made arrangements to "graft" us into his own family, we took everyone through an experiential lesson on what "grafting" really means, using real branches from a shrub and information we learned from an employee at a tree farm.

7. Jesus and Satan's Family

We targeted this class to explore what we could learn from Jesus' relationship with Satan. We gathered everyone's preconceptions about Satan and his demons and then used film clips from *The Lion King*, *Amadeus*, and *Rain Man* as sparks to start everyone thinking about the forces that shaped Satan, how he lives out his hatred of God, and how Jesus related to him. Then we dived into the many ways Jesus set out to "destroy the works of the devil."

8. Jesus and His True Mission

Was Jesus focused on us or on his Father when he agreed to leave heaven and enter into our world as a baby? In this class we drilled into what we really know about Jesus' true mission on earth and introduced a way of understanding his mission through the lens of story, rather than the lens of propositional truth. We watched a long scene from *Les Miserables*, one of the greatest films ever made, about a heroic figure who rescues a hopeless prostitute from her hellish life. We challenged participants to "mine" truths from the story that would help us understand Jesus' mission.

9. Jesus Acting Supernaturally

What's the point of Jesus walking on water, anyway? We prodded everyone to reexamine Jesus' supernatural actions through the lens of the train scene from *Spider-Man 2*. We hopscotched through a bunch of Scripture passages that showed Jesus acting supernaturally and then asked small groups to answer the big question for their assigned passage: "What does Jesus want us to know about him—and about his Father—through these supernatural acts?"

10. Jesus the Slaughtered Lamb

We took the defining quote for this class from the last *Lord of the Rings* film—*The Return of the King*. In a powerful interchange between the elf king Elrond and the heroic Aragorn, the two repeat an ancient creed of kings: "I give hope to men;

I keep none for myself." We used art, a film clip, and an experiential quest for "slaughtered lamb" parables to explore Jesus' role as the slaughtered lamb.

11. Jesus, Post-Resurrection

In this class we played detective to unravel the reasons behind Jesus' curious behavior after his resurrection. We gave each table a different post-resurrection Jesus story and then asked them to use these questions to explore the story: Why did Jesus say these things? Why did Jesus do these things? Why did others react to Jesus the way they did? Then we gathered each table's responses and prodded people to push back against any pat answers.

12. Jesus as the Hub of Your Life

We used this class to do an overview of our summer journey and closely examined the handoff of the baton from Jesus to the Holy Spirit after his resurrection (the greatest relay team ever assembled). We ended with a simple but profound question: "What's the difference, if any, between being a Christian and being a Christ follower?"

In the next-to-last class of this 12-part series, we announced that we still planned to end the class the following week (we'd been asked several times to extend the class into the fall). We were startled by the response—so many people were literally begging us to keep it going. Now, we felt like we'd worked hard and listened hard to God as we prepared our Pursuit, but of course the class still had many flaws. I think the reason people felt so strongly about continuing was simply that they'd drunk more deeply than ever before of Jesus—not to get something from him, but to enjoy him. And like a Lay's potato chip, once you've tasted Jesus you won't settle for just one taste of him. This is exactly why "Who do I say Jesus is?" is such a foundational question—it sets the stage for an obsessive pursuit of him, and once you get kids doing that, they'll be hooked by him alone, not what he can do for them.

You know discipleship is happening when kids do what Peter did in the aftermath of Jesus' least popular sermon (in John 6). When Jesus told the crowds they'd have to "eat his flesh and drink his blood" to have any part of him, the adoring crowds suddenly thought better of following him. Then Jesus turned to his best friends and asked them if they were going to leave, too. Peter responded (and I absolutely love this) by saying, "Where else would we go, Lord? You alone have words of life and truth."

That's a ruined-for-Jesus disciple talking.

JESUS REVEALED GOD BY FORCING HIS DISCIPLES TO DEPEND ON HIM

Interviewing Leonard Sweet is one of the great perks of my job. Leonard is a professor of evangelism at Drew University and author of many acclaimed books,

ON TEACHING TEENAGERS THE FAITH

In an address to the Catholic Church's 8th International Youth Forum, Harvard law professor Mary Ann Glendon said: "If religious formation does not come up to the general level of secular education, we are going to run into trouble defending our beliefs—even to ourselves. We are going to feel helpless when we come up against the secularism and relativism that are so pervasive in our culture and in the university. We are going to be tongue-tied when our faith comes under unjust attack."[1]

The churches studied in the *Exemplary Youth Ministries* project couldn't agree more, and they're doing something about it:

- "Here we talk about everyday situations, like, you can pick out things happening at school and they can help you relate scripture to everyday life."
  —A teenager at First United Methodist Church in Valparaiso, Indiana
- " 'Our real responsibility is in discipleship to help [our young people] discover what their faith is like—not mine, not the pastor's, not their parents.'
  The point of our youth group is, 'How does your faith attach to your life?' 'How do your decisions reflect your relationship with God?' "
  —Kerry Gruizenga, youth minister at First Presbyterian Church in Billings, Montana
- "We talk about things that matter…We talk about how to talk about your faith, world religions, and our own questions about faith."
  —A teenager at Thornapple Evangelical Covenant Church in Grand Rapids, Michigan
- "The genius behind [the ministry] is that they're intentional about going deep and they've replicated with others who can share the burden with them. They've purposely done that instead of being biggest, flashiest, showiest. The purpose here is going deep."
  —A parent at Newport Mesa Christian Center in Costa Mesa, California

---

1 This is from a prepared address by Harvard Law professor Mary Ann Glendon for the Pontifical Council for the Laity's 8th International Youth Forum, held near Rome in April 2004.

including *SoulTsunami*, *AquaChurch*, *SoulSalsa*, and *The Gospel According to Starbucks*. He's a theologian-futurist-teacher-preacher-innovator-catalyst. In fact, Len wins my personal award for "Person Deserving of Most Hyphens in Bio." I met Len many moons ago when he was speaking at the Princeton Forums on Youth Ministry.

Here's a snippet from one of our conversations. It drills into the last point on my road map to Jesus-centered discipleship—plunging teenagers into real responsibilities that force them to depend on God.

RL: Talk about some of the stumbling blocks an adult might see in handing over ministry to young people.

Sweet: There's been a radical shift in learning styles. Most adults learned by trial and error; teenagers learn by trial and success. In other words, we were taught that until we can get it right, don't do it. Until you get all your right beliefs down, until you understand this thing fully, you can't participate in ministry. For these trial-and-success kids, there's no concept of error. They learn by doing. How do you become a disciple of Jesus? You learn by doing. So the church has got to have a greater toleration for mistakes, falls, failures, misconceptions, and miscues. Young people will learn to be leaders by doing it.

RL: I think many churches have a huge fear about kids having no concept of error. They fear that kids don't know right from wrong, and the statistics seem to back them up...So when you say kids have no concept of error and it's OK to let them learn by doing, that raises red flags.

Sweet: Moderns define truth propositionally. Postmoderns define truth relationally. This is huge. The truth is...both. Truth is part proposition. But let me tell you, postmoderns are helping us rediscover the way in which truth is relational. Jesus didn't say, "Come follow me and I'll give you propositions." No, he said, "I am the way."

Biblical truth is a relationship. The modern world lost that. We boiled down biblical truth to four spiritual laws. That's how we tried to lead people to Christ. No. These kids are so right about this—truth is fundamentally defined in relationship terms. Jesus, who majored in relationships with the disciples and others, did teach doctrine. But the propositions came in the context of a walk with a person. God didn't send us a set of propositions, God sent us a person. And it's the person of Jesus.[10]

Essentially, Sweet is saying today's Millennials are learn-as-they-do teenagers. Well, I think Jesus loves the "challenge me" spirit of today's teenagers. When it

---

10 This conversation is excerpted from an interview with Leonard Sweet published in the article "Second Century Youth Ministry," in the September/October 1999 issue of Group Magazine.

came time to cement what he'd been teaching and modeling for his disciples, he sent them out in pairs to "heal, cast out demons, and preach good news to the captives." He didn't wait until he was sure they had it right before he tossed them into the work of ministry.

In fact, you could make a pretty good case that they never "got it right," even after the Holy Spirit arrived to empower them after Jesus' ascension. Peter and Paul fought over their different approaches to ministry and relationships. The churches they planted struggled with sexual improprieties, petty squabbles that led to civil lawsuits, and an addiction to "works" as a form of earning grace, among many other problems. There was nothing perfect about the early disciples and nothing perfect about what they planted. But nevertheless, here you and I are—direct examples of "fruit" from their 2,000-year-old labors.

Jesus understood that all fruit is produced by acts of faith—Paul wrote in Hebrews 11:6 that "without faith it is impossible to please God." It requires little faith to simply hear the truth, but we're forced into faith when we act on it. The church was established and spread on the impetus of countless acts of imperfect faith. And the adults and teenagers enjoying life in the 21 "exemplary" youth ministries targeted in the study have made an art form of throwing "imperfect kids" into significant ministry responsibilities:

- The Rev. Dave Byrum says that his congregation has "tied its wagon to the youth" and points out that every great revival in America was led by young people. He makes sure to intentionally include "young people and youth ministry in the major decision steps of our congregation. We invite our youth to be a part of our visioning and implementation."
- Johnny Derouen, who's now teaching at Southwestern Baptist Theological Seminary after a long stretch of leading the youth ministry at Travis Avenue Baptist Church in Fort Worth, Texas, says, "My job is to teach the students and adults and parents...I teach them how to do ministry and I let them do ministry...I give it back to them and it is their ministry...As a team we can do it. The high school students are trained at school to do things by themselves and I'm not going to do it for them when they get here. I will learn more preparing to teach and the goal is to get them to teach themselves...The whole program is geared to push you to the next level...By the time you are a junior or senior you are leading the program, you're leading small groups, mission trip groups, you're running the programs. You don't have to, but it is expected. I feel it leads to maturity."
- An adult volunteer at New Colony Baptist Church in Billerica, Massachusetts, says: "We had students writing their own psalms. And one of our youth leaders put it to music and made a whole CD of kids' songs." Another volunteer leader adds, "The kids take such ownership—they plan and help with the art worship and then lead the rest of the group

in the worship. They've made songs, a movie. We're doing an experience tomorrow—it's not us standing in front of them telling them what to say and what to do."

- A teenage girl at Newport Mesa Christian Center in Costa Mesa, California, once wrote, as a joke, that she'd like to play cowbell during the worship time. "I was totally kidding. But next week Lynette [the youth pastor] gave me a cow bell and I was playing during worship. I didn't even know how to play. If you want to lead clapping during worship, they will make a place for you."

I could go on and on with "youth ownership" comments from people serving at every level in these exemplary youth ministries—these represent just a sample. It's startling how passionately committed they all are to equipping kids for the work of ministry and then releasing them into real responsibilities.

It's interesting that youth-led ministry is really the thing that sparked "youth ministry" in the first place, way back in 1881 when Christian Endeavor was founded by Francis Clark. In his day, teenagers "weren't considered serious enough to make the same commitment to Christ as adults." On February 2, 1881, Clark decided to modify the "temperance pledge"—a commitment to *not do* something—and created a two-page list of things a young Christian *could do* to live his or her relationship with Christ in everyday life.

According to Christian Endeavor: "The 57 young people of the Williston Congregational Church of Portland, Maine were stunned by the level of commitment Clark asked of them. This meant a *real* sacrifice of time and energy. They would *actually* have to *live* the Christian life. They weren't sure they could do it—neither was Clark's own wife Harriet. But with encouragement from the Sunday school teacher, William Pennel, every single person signed. The results were astonishing. The young people took ownership of their Christianity. They led Bible studies, professed their faith publicly, and applied Christianity to every area of their lives. Their churches grew, the ranks of mission organizations swelled, and their cause circled the globe."[11]

What Clark did was Christ-like and Jesus-centered at its core. So, in the spirit of WDJD, let's look more closely at *how* Jesus plunged his disciples into their "imperfect faith" adventures and what he did after they returned. We'll use Matthew 10 and 11 as a sort of template—not to extract a Jesus formula for launching kids into significant responsibilities, but to yield ourselves to our beloved Mentor.

1. He conferred on them the spiritual authority they needed to do the job. "He called his twelve disciples to him and gave them authority to drive out evil spirits and to heal every disease and sickness" (Matthew 10:1).

---

11 This information was gleaned from the Christian Endeavor Web site at www.christianendeavor.com.

How is the way we ask teenagers to step up and fill important responsibilities any different from the way their teachers, coaches, or employers ask them to do the same? Well, it's unlikely any of them would lay hands on them and formally confer spiritual authority on them. The point is to publicly recognize that they've been called out or "set apart" for these responsibilities and that they won't be doing their work under their own authority or power. The book *Judaism for Dummies* describes the Hebrew word *s'michah*—the laying on of hands—this way: "S'michah is a way of conferring the authority of leadership from one person to another. First seen in Moses' transferring leadership of the Hebrews to Joshua just prior to entering the Holy Land, s'micha now refers to ordaining rabbis (where the laying on of hands is still performed)."[12]

2. *He started them out with a doable challenge.* "These twelve Jesus sent out with the following instructions: 'Do not go among the Gentiles or enter any town of the Samaritans. Go rather to the lost sheep of Israel' " (Matthew 10:5–6).

Rather than forcing them into a cross-cultural challenge or an environment of stiff resistance, Jesus starts them off in familiar surroundings with familiar people. Later on they'll go "to the ends of the earth," but for now the challenge needs to be small enough to ensure some level of success.

When I was learning how to be a street evangelist in Europe (even now I'm amazed I really did that when I was young), our trainers started us off by teaching us a discussion-starting drama we could perform to attract a crowd. The first place we did it was a public piazza in Rome that was well known as a gathering place for young people interested in conversation with Americans. We did the drama, and it provided an easy way to strike up a conversation with strangers. The bridge from shy, scared, awkward guy to international missionary was relatively easy because my leaders understood how to give us doable challenges.

3. *He gave them specific boundaries for their responsibilities.* "As you go, preach this message: 'The kingdom of heaven is near.' Heal the sick, raise the dead, cleanse those who have leprosy, drive out demons" (Matthew 10:7-8a).

If we're releasing kids to thrive in their responsibilities, they'll need specific expectations from us. Jesus went so far as to tell his disciples exactly what he wanted them to say and gave them four ministry responsibilities that very definitely required them to depend on the power of God. He also, by the way, spent a lot of time modeling these responsibilities, giving them plenty of time to learn how to do them from an incredible Mentor.

4. *He told them to expect God to meet their needs along the way.* "Freely you have received, freely give. Do not take along any gold or silver or copper in your belts; take no

---

12 Taken from Appendix A of *Judaism for Dummies* by Rabbi Ted Falcon and David Blatner (New York: Hungry Minds, Inc., 2001).

bag for the journey, or extra tunic, or sandals or a staff; for the worker is worth his keep (Matthew 10:8b-10).

Jesus understood that ministry is all about generosity—we give out of generous hearts, and we receive from God's generous heart. That means we ask teenagers to give out of the fullness of what they've received and trust God to give them "manna" for their basic needs. A teenage girl at Newport Mesa Christian Center, an exemplary youth ministry, told an interviewer, "We see other [leaders] and how close they are to God and we realize we can do it too."

5. He told them to look for people who were open to what they had to give. "Whatever town or village you enter, search for some worthy person there and stay at his house until you leave. As you enter the home, give it your greeting. If the home is deserving, let your peace rest on it; if it is not, let your peace return to you. If anyone will not welcome you or listen to your words, shake the dust off your feet when you leave that home or town" (Matthew 10:11-14).

Greg Stier once told me that he was walking in downtown Denver when he came across a couple of street evangelists who were screaming fire-and-brimstone invectives at passersby. Because he felt a kinship with them as a fellow passionate evangelist, Greg approached them, introduced himself, and asked how things were going, screaming-wise. The two eagerly shared that they'd been experiencing a lot of "persecution" for what they were doing but were committed to keep on doing it. Greg responded, "You're being persecuted because you're behaving like jerks!" Then he challenged them to try a more relational, people-honoring strategy. He turned and saw a businessman approaching on the sidewalk. He caught his eye and asked, "How's it going?" Because he asked the question seriously, the guy stopped and entered into conversation with him. Greg gradually looped the conversation toward Jesus, and the man eventually left with a smile on his face. The lesson, he said, is to learn how to sense openness in people and then respectfully move toward them with anticipation.

6. He told them to expect trouble and not be surprised when it came. "Be on your guard against men; they will hand you over to the local councils and flog you in their synagogues" (Matthew 10:17).

Joani Schultz, co-author of *Kids Taking Charge: Youth-Led Ministry* and the chief creative officer where I work, says: "Anyone contemplating a movement toward youth-led ministry must weigh this approach's dangers and pitfalls. It's definitely not the easiest way to do youth ministry. But then, few things of value come easily. Treat failure as one of your most trusted teachers."[13]

7. He showed his trust in them by not shadowing them as they ventured into the unknown. "After Jesus had finished instructing his twelve disciples, he went on from there to teach and preach in the towns of Galilee" (Matthew 11:1).

---

13 This comment originally appeared in "The Do's and Don'ts of Youth-Led Ministry," from the September/October 2006 issue of Group Magazine.

After Jesus had delivered his instructions to the disciples, he took off on his own ministry trip. Talk about communicating trust! Effectively, he was telling them he wasn't at all worried or anxious about how they'd fare on their adventure. I like how Joani Schultz frames the "price" we pay for handing off ministry responsibilities to teenagers: "Youth ministry is not about us; it's about God's passion for growing disciples. We must be willing to relinquish much of the leadership spotlight to allow kids to 'dance' (and sometimes suffer) in its glow. Young people are the visible doers. We're the humble servants. We're involved in youth ministry not for our own glory, but to satisfy a Christ-like craving to see young people grow into God's dream for them."[14]

And that growing does come with a price—part of it means we give over our very human need to receive glory. I once asked a roomful of youth pastors this question: "If you were guaranteed that you'd make a life-changing difference in a teenager's life but were also guaranteed that you'd never get a thank you for it, would you do it?" Every hand in the place shot up—it was unanimous. I just love the spirit of self-sacrifice among youth leaders.

8. He helped his disciples debrief their ministry adventures after they returned.

Luke records Jesus sending out 72 of his followers (Luke 10) to heal people and cast out demons. When they returned they said, "Lord, even the demons submit to us in your name." And Jesus jumped into his debriefing: "I saw Satan fall like lightning from heaven. I have given you authority to trample on snakes and scorpions and to overcome all the power of the enemy; nothing will harm you. However, do not rejoice that the spirits submit to you, but rejoice that your names are written in heaven."

He's basically reminding them the power they experienced on their adventure came directly from him (so don't get too impressed with yourselves) and the power to cast out demons is nothing compared to the reality that God had adopted them into his family. He's simply using a powerful experience as the context to teach and frame the truth.

In the end, the practice of youth-led ministry creates a saturating counterculture that raises expectations for everyone in the ministry. It's the perfect table setter for mentoring relationships—when kids are working together with adults to do something great, mentoring happens organically. But that's a topic for the next chapter.

---

14 This comment originally appeared in "The Do's and Don'ts of Youth-Led Ministry," from the September/October 2006 issue of Group Magazine.

Mentoring

(WITH AN INTRODUCTION BY BO BOSHERS
AND JUDSON POLING)

BRICK-WALL MENTORING

When I first started in youth ministry, we planned an outreach event every Tuesday night. After the program was over, the leadership team—a dozen high school and college kids—gathered in the parking lot by a low brick wall. It wasn't a planned meeting; we simply gravitated to that wall. At first a parade of young people who'd attended that night would file by to say hi and introduce their friends. Later, after everyone else had said goodnight, I'd be standing next to that wall with my five key leaders: Coleman, Dave, Troy, Trevor, and Alex. We were always the last to leave, patiently waiting for our savored storytelling time to begin.

We told such a wide variety of stories—from funny to touching. We laughed about what went wrong that night, how bad the music was, mistakes in the drama, something I said in the message that didn't make sense, or something that happened during the sports competition.

Then the mood changed and the stories shifted from the evening's activities to the changed lives of kids. Maybe one of my leaders had been praying for months that a friend would come and that friend had finally shown up—and loved it. Or maybe another would talk about a God-centered conversation with a teenager who was, for the first time, exploring a relationship with Jesus.

We had fantastic celebrations when we found out a student had prayed to receive Christ.

I remember looking at these young men, listening to their stories, and thinking: "This is what I want to give my life to. This is what really matters to me." I felt incredibly fulfilled every time I looked into their eyes and saw their compassion, their commitment, and their love for God. Sitting on that brick wall, right there in an empty parking lot, God showed me what ministry was all about. I could put up with all the other "stuff" of youth ministry for that payoff.

More than 20 years later, I still love "sitting on the brick wall," looking into the eyes of a few teenagers I know and love well and seeing their passion, their desire, their ambition to change the world.

WAS JESUS A SUCCESS?

Let's leave that brick wall and go back in time to look at Jesus' ministry through the "success filter" we commonly use in ministry today. Granted, Jesus drew some large crowds at the height of his popularity. But only 120 were gathered in the upper room a few weeks after his death—not the huge crowds who'd cheered his triumphal entry into Jerusalem or the thousands who'd flocked to hear him on the hillsides. Where did they all go? His looked more like a ministry in decline, maybe even dead in the water, than a movement destined to shake up the world.

Despite all these earmarks of failure, Jesus unabashedly proclaimed he'd completed what his father sent him to do (John 17:4). So by Jesus' measure of success (whatever it was), he'd made it. He said he'd accomplished all his goals.

What explains this discrepancy? We can find the answer by reflecting on Jesus' ministry using a different plumb line (Amos 7:7). Rather than focus on his declining numbers, take a close look at the depth of impact he made on a few key individuals.

Jesus was the catalyst for deep personal transformation in those who followed him—hang around him long enough and you'd find your life radically altered. We believe the standard by which Jesus measured his own success—and how we ought to also measure our success—was deep, lasting change in a few. Dallas Willard says, "Christians must be weighed, not just counted." The disciples were so altered by Jesus' life and teaching that they gave the rest of their natural lives to perpetuating his work. In our surface-oriented culture, wouldn't results like this be a refreshing change?

MINISTRY AT BOTH ENDS OF THE FUNNEL

The simple truth is that Jesus had it right. His focus was always on relationships, and his ministry was in perfect balance. He gathered and spoke to crowds, but never allowed their size or adulation to trick him into thinking he'd done his work. Rather, while speaking and ministering to the many, he also found a few young men and women to invest in deeply. Under the influence and power of the Holy Spirit, that band of followers "turned the world upside down" (Acts 17:6). We desperately need that to happen again.

At the "wide end of the funnel," Jesus attracted a loose following of many. And at a certain point, after a night of prayer, he gathered a select few and appointed them to "be with him" (Mark 3:14). Though public miracles and teaching would be the most obvious aspect of his ministry, his deep work with a few—the narrow end of the funnel—set the stage for an earth-shaking movement.

At the heart of any ministry that seeks to emulate Jesus—no matter how expansive or public its outward manifestation may be—must be a commitment from the leaders to mentor a few in the daily aspects of living. We call that the Be-With Factor. Jesus lived it, and it's God's call on everyone who follows in his steps. It means mentoring is by far the most rewarding activity for anyone who cares about young people. Whatever else you do, commit to "being with" a few so that lasting life change happens.

—BO BOSHERS
Executive Director of Student Ministries for the Willow Creek Association
—JUDSON POLING
Small Group Leader at Willow Creek Church, Author and Editor

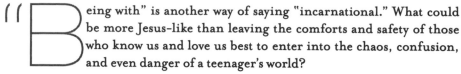"eing with" is another way of saying "incarnational." What could be more Jesus-like than leaving the comforts and safety of those who know us and love us best to enter into the chaos, confusion, and even danger of a teenager's world?

Not long ago I read about an Indiana youth pastor named Scott Greene who decided to go back to high school as a student for two weeks. He went through all the hoops with school administrators, signed up for classes (including gym), and tried to experience everything a typical student would. Those two weeks changed the way Greene sees his ministry to teenagers, and it grabbed the attention of the national media.

I contacted Scott and asked him to write about his experience for Group Magazine. In his setup to the article, Scott said: "I've pushed school lunches and campus visits off my calendar more times than I can remember [because of insecurity and fear]. I've invented excuses to avoid them, intentionally scheduled over them, and even driven all the way to the school and simply not gone in. But I've paid the price for it. After 10 years in youth ministry, I realized my 'avoidance strategies' had left me nearly out of touch with today's youth culture. My passion to reach young people was as strong as ever, but my ability to understand their world was quickly evaporating. As much as I love serving God in youth ministry, I'd rather listen to NPR than watch MTV. The older I get, the less empathetic I can be towards teenagers, their culture, and their everyday predicaments. So I knew I needed to do something radical to reverse my momentum."[1]

And that "something" was to do a belly-flop off the incarnational diving board, right into the thick of his teenagers' real world—the only place a mentor can really make an impact. In another stretch of thought-provoking conversation, Len Sweet and I talked about the heart of mentoring and why teenagers are so impacted by it:

> RL: Let's say you've got a traditional youth ministry model that has a charismatic leader at its center—that person is the focal point for young people and for the adult leaders who help in the ministry...What are the changes that must happen for youth leaders who suspect there's a better way to do ministry?
>
> Sweet: The biggest one is their need to give up the ministry. I tell youth pastors, "Your major job is to give away the ministry to your kids. You must decrease that Christ may increase in their lives." These kids need mentors. They do not need pied pipers.
>
> This is the first generation in history that does not need authority figures to access information. But wait a minute—they need authority figures all the more to process all that information. They don't need us

---

1   This comment originally appeared in Scott Greene's article "Lessons From a Thirtysomething Sophomore," in the September/October 2006 issue of Group Magazine.

to get the truth—what they need is mentoring. "Now that I can get it, help me. How do I live it? How do I perform it? How do I pray it?" That's the mentoring model. It's much more low-key but high-powered.

You can learn this from Star Wars, for cryin' out loud. These Jedi knights are spiritual masters. That's what we need—knights of faith that can show our kids what it means to be a master of the spiritual disciplines, a master of the spiritual life, a master of what it means to be a disciple of Jesus.[2]

Are you a "spiritual master" to your kids? Leave it to Len to set the bar high. But his insights are shot through with truth. Not long ago I created a survey I nicknamed "The Cool Youth Leader" and gave it to more than 15,000 Christian kids. I was after answers to a basic question: "What do you really want in a youth leader?" I asked them 28 questions, loosely organized around four umbrella characteristics: relational, spiritual, leadership, and personal. Their collective responses affirmed what's truest and best about youth ministers today and skewer the stereotypes.

The overall top four characteristics teenagers chose for their "dream" youth leader were:

1. *Creates a welcoming, friendly atmosphere for youth group activities—89 percent*
2. *Really listens well—88 percent*
3. *I can trust him or her when I have a problem and need advice—87 percent*
4. *Seems to notice and understand who I really am—81 percent*[3]

Notice a pattern here? I asked my friend Jeanne Mayo (who authored the introduction to Chapter 8, on small groups) to look at the results of the survey and give me her take on it. She said: "Voltaire said it well when he wrote, 'The ears are the gateway to the heart.' Youth leaders who train themselves to ask caring questions, avoid TRT (typical religious talk), and listen more than they talk will be powerful influences in their kids' lives."[4]

Simply put, I think our ability to listen well to young people, and then offer wise feedback, is our most important personal skill. And it's what fuels powerful, life-changing mentoring—that's exactly what kids say they're looking for in a mentor. Nine out of 10 kids in our survey said they're longing for a youth leader "who really listens well" and is "trustworthy when I have a problem and need

---

2 This conversation is excerpted from an interview published in "Second Century Youth Ministry," from the September/October 1999 issue of Group Magazine.

3 This study was conducted with more than 10,000 Christian teenagers attending Group workcamps during the summer of 2005. The results were published in "What Kids Really Want," from the January/February 2006 issue of Group Magazine.

4 Jeanne Mayo's comments are taken from "What Kids Really Want," from the January/February 2006 issue of Group Magazine.

advice." And almost three-quarters (71 percent) said they want a leader who "can handle my doubts, struggles, and strong emotions." Teenagers are trying to say they're really longing for adults who will listen well and continue to pursue them, no matter what.

Listening may be the most appreciated but least practiced skill in youth ministry—really, in every area of life. So here are two great questions to ask yourself the next time you're talking with a teenager in any setting:

- *"Would this young person say I'm riveted by him/her in this moment?"*
- *"What interior and exterior distractions do I need to set aside to rivet my attention right now?"*

I'll never forget a story I heard told by Frank Peretti, author of the mega-popular book *This Present Darkness* and many others, about his brutal years as a teenager. Because of a disfiguring medical condition when he was young, Peretti was bullied and mocked and shunned by his peers. One night, sitting by himself at youth group and contemplating how he might commit suicide that very night, Peretti was approached by an adult volunteer who offered him riveting attention. Six words helped change his life: "How you doing? You feeling OK?" Peretti was used to throwaway questions like these, so he brushed them off. But the volunteer stayed put, clearly not intending to move on until Peretti offered a real answer. He asked again. And the leverage of that adult's riveted attention cracked open the door to Peretti's tormented soul—he broke down and shared everything with the volunteer and found a tiny ledge of hope to stand on.

It's amazing to me how the little things—making sure we're listening with riveted attention when kids are talking to us—can mean the difference between life and death.

Five years ago I created a questionnaire I called the "Cool Church Survey"—a precursor to the "Cool Youth Leader Survey" I've already mentioned. I wanted to know why Christian teenagers commit to, or stay committed to, a church. Out of a long list of factors I asked them to rate, the top vote-getter was "A welcoming atmosphere where [I] can be myself."[5]

Five years later they answered the same way in our "Cool Youth Leader Survey." Four out of five (81 percent) say it matters a lot to them to have a youth leader "who seems to notice and understand who I really am." And nine out of 10 (89 percent) say they want a youth leader "who creates a welcoming, friendly atmosphere for youth group activities"—kids voted this the most important characteristic in our survey. All this highlights an overriding truth about our approach to mentoring—kids fundamentally long to belong, and Jesus-like mentoring creates an environment of belonging. Jesus' disciples—those he mentored—"belonged"

---

5 This study was conducted with more than 10,000 Christian teenagers attending Group workcamps during the summer of 2000. The results were published in "The Cool Church," from the May/June 2001 issue of Group Magazine.

so deeply that all of them were martyred because they refused to place their own lives above their identity as Christ followers.

POSITIVE LABELING

I think powerful mentoring involves practicing a skill I call Positive Labeling. It's a principle I drew from a "beeline" to Jesus, based on Christ's example in Matthew 16 when Jesus told Peter: "I also say to you that you are Peter, and upon this rock I will build My church; and the gates of Hades will not overpower it" (NASB).

I think Jesus was pinpointing the second big question that a Jesus-centered youth ministry helps kids answer—"Who does Jesus say I am?" As we more and more "name" Jesus for who he really is, he names *us* for who we really are. Jesus is so generous—he wants to reveal to us who we are and what we were made to do. One of the profound purposes of youth ministry is to create the right setting and circumstances for kids to experience Jesus unveiling them.

In J. R. R. Tolkien's powerful conclusion to the *Lord of the Rings* saga—*The Return of the King*—the man who's spent his life as a ranger, the man who calls himself Strider, must step into his true role as King of Gondor—the king who will lead the forces of good against the forces of evil. Because of the shame he feels over the cowardice of his ancestors, Aragorn has deftly avoided embracing his identity as king—it's as if he's afraid to become what he was meant to be. But then a wise older man—sorry, older elf—calls him out.

In one of the film's climactic scenes, Aragorn is summoned to a tent, where he sees King Theoden talking with a hooded figure, the elfin Lord Elrond. He's there to challenge Aragorn to embrace his true identity because the fate of the world hangs on his leadership. Elrond hands Aragorn a sword called Anduril—a legendary weapon wielded by the great kings of Gondor. I'll let the film's actual screenplay pick up the story:

> Aragorn: (*Takes the sword, staring at it in wonder.*) Sauron will not have forgotten the sword of Elendil. (*He draws the long blade from its sheath.*) The blade that was broken shall return to Minas Tirith.
> Elrond: The man who can wield the power of this sword can summon to him an army more deadly than any that walks this earth. (*Elrond stares hard at Aragorn.*) Put aside the Ranger—become who you were born to be—take the Dimholt Road. (*A heavy silence hangs in the room.*) [6]

Of course, in the story Aragorn goes on to assume the mantle of king and lead the forces of good to victory over Sauron and the forces of darkness. When I show this powerful scene to youth pastors, I ask them to pinpoint what

---

6 Dialogue taken from the shooting script for *The Lord of the Rings: The Return of the King*, written by Fran Walsh, Philippa Boyens, and Peter Jackson, based on the book by J. R. R. Tolkien.

Elrond said that forced a turning point in Aragorn's life. The answer: Elrond told Aragorn who he really was and challenged him to step fully into his true identity. Has God ever answered this overshadowing question in your life? I mean, when have you sensed him telling you who you really are?

I remember my "Aragorn moment" so well. It was a little over 10 years ago. I was speaking at a youth ministry conference—the last place I wanted to be at that moment in my life. My wife and I were in the throes of a significant challenge to our young marriage. I'd left for the speaking trip upset and worried—I could sense our relationship was in some danger, and it was killing me. I mean I literally felt like someone was repeatedly jamming a dagger into my gut.

I walked through the halls of the convention center hoping no one would recognize me so I wouldn't have to talk with anyone. My interior conversation was full of accusations and criticisms—all directed at myself (maybe a *few* at my wife).

It was during one of my wall-hugging walks down a crowded hallway that I felt God breaking through my defenses and helping me to understand better the emotions and thoughts running through my mind. He spoke to me like a lightning bolt. It seemed so clear that I had to step into an empty room and write it all down as the words came gushing at me. I couldn't have been more shocked (and embraced) by what I sensed—here's what I wrote down:

> I'm a quarterback. I see the field. I'm squirming away from the rush to find space to release the ball. I never give up. I have courage in the face of ferocity—in fact, ferocity draws out my courage. I want to score even when the team is too far behind for it to matter. I love the thrill of creating a play in the huddle, under pressure, and spreading the ball around to everyone on the team. I have no greater feeling than throwing the ball hard to a spot and watching the receiver get to it without breaking stride. In fact, I love it most when the receiver is closely covered and it takes a perfect throw to get it to him. I have the same feeling when I throw a bomb and watch the receiver run under it, or when I tear away from the grasp of a defender, or when I see and feel blood on my elbows or knees and feel alive because of it. I love to score right after the other team has scored, but I want to do it methodically, first down by first down, right down the field. I love fourth down! I want to win but am satisfied by fighting well.

Now, I've never put this in print before—reading it again I realize how deeply it still resonates with me, 10 years after my crisis (by the way, my wife and I made it through that time—God used its brutal leverage to bring radical and beautiful change into our marriage). Of course, "quarterback" is just a metaphor for something much more pertinent and treasured: the true nature of my heart and identity. God was describing me as I *really* am, and he did it at a desperate moment in my life. As the years go by I yield, more and more, to my true identity.

I know "labeling" is politically incorrect and akin to a sin in our culture today, but God is calling us—as mentors and people who recruit and train mentors—to vigorously, passionately, positively label our kids. Positive Labeling is the key to helping them to hear from Jesus about who they really are.

The point here is not simply to become more affirming—though most affirmation isn't a bad thing, of course. Affirmation is designed to make someone feel good about who they are. The skill of Positive Labeling is designed to reveal to a person his or her true nature. The goal is to pay attention to what God is doing in your teenagers, identify it, and name it—to help them hear how Jesus describes them.

ANSWERING THE QUESTION

The first practical thing we can do is simply help kids find the answer to this life-changing question—"Who does Jesus say I am?" Find a place to do this where kids can have some quiet space—where they can have a sense of safety and isolation. Some youth workers have told me this works very well on a retreat. The key is to do this at a time when kids are naturally at a lower energy level and to make sure they have the physical and emotional space they need to feel "alone."

They'll need something to write on and with. Then, in the quiet, have them simply ask Jesus: "Who do you say I am?" Have them write what they hear. Assure them that they won't have to share any of this with others unless they want to. Remind them that it's possible they may not hear anything from God at this time—that's OK, too. Finally, before they ask Jesus this question, instruct them to do two things: "Tell God you want him to silence your own voice, and then ask him to silence the voice of his enemy." Then have them sit quietly and ask Jesus the question—"Who do you say I am?"

Again, it's a good idea for you and your volunteer leaders to do this before you ask your kids to do it.

After kids finish this activity, form small groups with at least one adult leader in each one. Ask those kids who'd like to share about their experience to do so in their small group. Then make your adult leaders available for private, one-on-one connection times for those kids who'd like to discuss the experience but don't want to do it in front of other teenagers.

ACTING LIKE SHERLOCK HOLMES

When you practice Positive Labeling with your kids, you'll have to learn to act like Sherlock Holmes in their lives—looking for evidence of their "real name." I mean, you'll need to learn (and teach your adult leaders) to pay attention to, and pounce on, little details about your kids. The goal is to solve the mystery of their purpose in God's kingdom—to set the stage for them to hear how God describes them.

I created a simple worksheet to help energize this process. It's called The Sherlock Holmes File (below). You simply choose a teenager in your group you know pretty well and then answer a few simple questions about that young person. Try it right now—plug a teenager's name into the worksheet and take a few minutes to fill it out.

THE SHERLOCK HOLMES FILE FOR

Student's Name: _____

1. Three things I've noticed that this student seems to love:
   -
   -
   -

2. Three ways I've seen this student contribute:
   -
   -
   -

3. One way I've experienced this student's strength:

4. When this student seems most alive, he/she is usually doing this:

5. One thing that this student does that seems to come easily is:

6. In the list of ministry needs below, mark all that are possibilities for him/her, based on the evidence you've collected so far.

   ❏ Worship Team   ❏ Evangelism Team
   ❏ Teaching Team   ❏ Communication Team
   ❏ Small-Group Leader   ❏ Web/Technology Team
   ❏ Visual Arts Team (Painting, Drawing, etc.) ❏ Recreation Leader
   ❏ Spoken-Arts Team (Drama, Poetry, etc.)   ❏ Hospitality/Welcome Team
   ❏ Physical Arts Team (Dance, Sports, etc.)   ❏ Prayer Team

7. Stop now to pray. Ask something like: "God, who do you say that this student is?" Write what you hear.

8. Now for the labeling part: Here's one thing about who Jesus has created this person to be that I'll speak out on a regular basis:

Now, this is a very powerful process and shouldn't be taken lightly. It's God who knows your kids' real name, and it's God who will reveal it to them. In Isaiah 43:1 (NASB) God says: "Do not fear, for I have redeemed you; I have called you by name; you are Mine!" This is not a process any of us should do alone—choose the person on your team who knows each young person best, and have that person fill this out. If no one knows a teenager well enough to fill out a sheet, that's telling you something. It's time to pursue.

As your team fills out these sheets, get together to discuss what you've learned. When all of you are doing this regularly, and you commit to communicating their "true identity" in a multitude of ways, your kids will be encouraged to consciously move toward who they really are and give what they have to give. This skill of Positive Labeling will infuse with power your mentoring—so make sure you train your adult

7 Taken from *Now Discover Your Strengths* by Marcus Buckingham and Donald Clifton (New York: Free Press, 2001).

THE WHEAT-AND-WEEDS IMPERATIVE

Marcus Buckingham and Donald Clifton, authors of the bestselling business book *Now Discover Your Strengths* popularized a profound truth that applies to the skill of Positive Labeling. It's a truth that's locked up in a strange little story Jesus told—the Parable of the Weeds in Matthew 13:

Jesus told them another parable: "The kingdom of heaven is like a man who sowed good seed in his field. But while everyone was sleeping, his enemy came and sowed weeds among the wheat, and went away. When the wheat sprouted and formed heads, then the weeds also appeared.

"The owner's servants came to him and said, 'Sir, didn't you sow good seed in your field? Where then did the weeds come from?'

" 'An enemy did this,' he replied.

"The servants asked him, 'Do you want us to go and pull them up?'

" 'No,' he answered, 'because while you are pulling the weeds, you may root up the wheat with them. Let both grow together until the harvest. At that time I will tell the harvesters: First collect the weeds and tie them in bundles to be burned; then gather the wheat and bring it into my barn.' "

Jesus is essentially saying, "Don't pay attention to the bad stuff—the weeds; instead, concentrate on nurturing the good stuff—I'll take care of the bad stuff later on." Buckingham and Clifton make the case that the best way to manage people is to discover their strengths and fuel them, not look for their weaknesses and try to remove or improve them. Companies that shift their attention from trying to attack their workers' weaknesses and instead concentrate on fueling their strengths, experience remarkable success.[7]

Translated to youth ministry, this new skill means we look for the kingdom of God in our kids and then speak it out to them...habitually and regularly. We recognize their "weeds," but we concentrate on growing their "wheat" instead. We help kids discover who they are, not who they're not.

leaders in it. In fact, every single adult in your ministry should consider himself or herself a mentor.

By the way, before you play with this idea, I suggest you fill out a Sherlock Holmes file for yourself and ask someone close to you to also fill it out for you. After both of you have filled out the sheet, compare what you've written. Then go to your favorite coffee shop or bakery or hot wings emporium and discuss two simple questions: What do we notice about the similarities between our lists—what stands out, and why? What do we notice about the differences between our lists—what stands out, and why?

When kids start to feel subtly and consistently saturated with true messages about their Jesus-fueled identity, they'll start saying things like teenagers at Rochester Covenant Church in Rochester, Minnesota, do. Listen to the impact of Positive Labeling on these "exemplary youth ministry" kids:

- *"Our leaders do a good job and really take the time to notice our gifts... I've gone out for coffee and they say, 'I've noticed you're really gifted in these areas.' That means so much more that they took the time to notice."*
- *"They don't just assign us to something."*
- *"When they tell you you're good at something, you're not just a number in the youth group. They are thinking about you and praying for you daily."*

These teenagers can actually articulate how well their adult leaders are mentoring them, and that means the message has sunk in—"You belong here, because we see you well."

Now that's the kind of community that will draw others into it.

Evangelism

(WITH AN INTRODUCTION BY GREG STIER)

RELIGIOUS PEOPLE RUBBED JESUS THE WRONG WAY, TOO

Years ago when I was a preaching pastor in Denver, Colorado, I used to go to the same restaurant every day to study for my sermons. I'd tank up on caffeine and the Spirit of God while hammering out my outlines and illustrations for the upcoming weekend services.

One day after a few hours of studying, I gathered my Bible and books, picked up my coffee-stained bill, and took my place in the way-too-long line to pay my bill (including a few extra dollars for tip/booth rental fees).

As I stood there, I felt somebody's eyes boring a hole through me. I turned to see a teenager staring at me with angry, hate-filled eyes. He looked to be about 16 years old—he was dressed completely in black, was covered in piercings, and had a snarl tattooed on his smirking face.

At first I didn't know what was going on, but then it hit me—this kid had been reading the words on the spines of the books tucked under my right arm. These were "Jesus books" and I could tell by the blaze in his gaze that this kid had a problem with that.

When our eyes met the situation got even more uncomfortable. The awkward moment led to his inevitable question, "Hey man, are you religious?"

I thought for a second and uttered, "I can't stand religious people—they make me want to puke."

"I can't stand them either!" he almost yelled. "They think they're better than everybody else!"

"Do you know who else couldn't stand them?" I asked.

"Who?" he answered.

"Jesus!" I shot back.

He looked surprised by my answer. "Are you serious?" he asked.

"I'm dead serious." I continued. "As a matter of fact, Jesus, the Son of God, came down from heaven to hang out with sinners like you and me, but the religious people got mad so they crucified him."

Now this kid started to get real worked up that the religious people crucified Jesus. So I continued: "But Jesus had the last laugh. Three days later he rose again from the dead, proving that he was God. Now he offers sinners like you and me eternal life if we simply trust in him."

By the time I was finished, this kid raised his fist into the air and shouted something like, "Jesus is awesome!"

For the first time in his young life, this counterculture teenager encountered the real, relevant, nonreligious, counterculture Jesus. It took just a few minutes to blow his lame mental image of the Son of God to tiny bits of stained-glass shrapnel.

We must do the same thing in our youth groups. Too many of our teenagers have never encountered the actual Jesus of the Bible. Too often their mental stereotype is the 6-foot-2-skinny-white-guy Jesus who loved peace, hated conflict, and did miracles.

But the Jesus of the Bible would be far too intense for the average church today. Building Jesus-centered evangelism into your youth ministry DNA means confronting teenagers with the Jesus they don't expect. The same Jesus that preached about heaven preached about hell even more. He is savior and judge, lion and lamb, compassion and intensity.

We must use the same bold, beautiful, catalytic, and contentious colors that the gospel writers used to paint him. When we do maybe our kids will thrust their fists into the air and for the first time proclaim, "Jesus is awesome!"

—GREG STIER
Founder and President of Dare 2 Share

How did you come to Christ? I'll bet your story is a lot like mine. My parents always took me to church when I was a kid, but every Sunday morning I prayed with all the fervor of Dwight L. Moody (I'm just assuming he was pretty good at praying) that they'd get up too late to cram us all into our Chevy station wagon—the one with the fake wood paneling on the sides—in time for church. I don't remember my parents ever sleeping in...not once.

Church was more boring than digging holes in our backyard. Whatever was going on there in that service, all I took from it was an increased ability to endure. But something really big happened the summer before fifth grade—my parents took me to see Pat Boone in concert at my town's rodeo grounds. The concert was only slightly better than backyard hole digging, but Pat did his best Four Spiritual Laws spiel and gave an invitation.

For some reason God captured me in that moment, and I headed down to the stage area to pray with a stranger while the blue-leisure-suited Pat crooned nearby. The gospel seemed simple to me, and the culture I lived in seemed to agree.

So maybe I was wrong about my coming-to-Christ story being a lot like yours—raise your hand if Pat Boone is your spiritual father...I thought so. Well, I was a dweeb then and I'm pretty much an older dweeb now. But my story got me wondering about the many diverse jungle paths people have taken through the wilderness to find Jesus (or more accurately, to be found by him). It's really amazing how unique every person's story is—from accidentally standing behind Greg Stier at a restaurant to accidentally letting yourself get dragged to a Pat Boone concert. But it makes sense to me when I think about Jesus as an artist.

Thomas Kinkade might paint some variation of the same cute-cottage-by-a-stream-with-a-bridge painting a million times, but Jesus would be more like Picasso—no two paintings remotely similar. That's because Jesus, like his Father, absolutely loves to create. Scientists estimate there are 1.75 million species in the world right now—they have to estimate because there are so many species, we can't even count them all.[1] Do we *need* 1.75 million species? Put another way, do we *need* every single one of those species—mosquitoes, for example? Nope and nope. But God created them anyway because he loves to create.

So, when I start to think about evangelism through the eyes of Jesus, I see the sensibilities of a jazz musician—in jazz there's a bass-line chord progression that serves as an anchor to an almost infinite array of creative "riffs" (to use my pastor Tom Melton's metaphor). Put another way, popular evangelism formulas—the Four Spiritual Laws and all its brood—are really the "riffs" of evangelism. I think we can discover the bass line of Jesus-centered evangelism by exploring it from both the perspective of the space shuttle and a dust mite.

THE VIEW FROM THE SPACE SHUTTLE

George Barna once wrote that his research showed the church was having "little evangelistic impact" on teenagers and adults and that the teenage years are not "prime years for evangelistic activity."[2] At the time, I thought these statements were ripe for rebuttal (I think I arrogantly said I'd "eat crow" if he was right), so I asked Dr. Dave Rahn of Huntington College and Youth for Christ, and members of the Association of Youth Ministry Educators, to partner with me to come up with our own small-scale research project to learn more about the role of youth ministry in Christian conversion. We designed a seven-question survey that youth ministry professors gave to 369 Christian students on 10 campuses across North America.[3] Here's what we discovered by examining evangelism from the stratosphere:

1. Jesus-centered evangelism is most often a marathon, not a sprint.
One linchpin question in our survey was: "When you think about how you came to faith in Christ, did it happen in an instant as it did with St. Paul, or did it happen over a longer period of time, as it did with St. Peter?" More than three quarters

---

1 Taken from the article "How Many Species Are There?" by the Environmental Literacy Council.

2 Taken from a November 1999 Barna research report on evangelistic impact in America.

3 All results and student comments in this chapter are from a survey co-created by Group Magazine, Dave Rahn, and the Association of Youth Ministry Educators and given to 369 Christian college students in the spring of 2000.

(77 percent) said their conversion was more like Peter's than Paul's, belying the moment-in-time conversion stereotype that dominates our thinking about evangelism.

So a lot of "the work of evangelism" looks a whole lot like "the work of discipleship"—we come alongside kids to invite them into our own intimate relationship with God, teach them the truth about Jesus and the kingdom of God, and then test their understanding by plunging them into experiences and responsibilities. These kids come to Christ the way Peter did—they have a startling encounter with Jesus, followed by a sort of "convert as you go" series of transforming experiences.

2. Jesus-centered evangelism looks more like a three-stage "launch vehicle" than a pop-bottle rocket.

Nine out of 10 of our survey respondents said they'd had "a crucial recommitment experience" that was as significant as their initial conversion. And two-thirds of these folks said their experience happened when they were teenagers. Kids can't get into a Christ-following orbit only from the force of their initial conversion any more than a pop-bottle rocket can break through the earth's atmosphere into space. They'll need to ride a launch vehicle that has several booster-rocket stages. And according to our survey, outreach trips, crises, big events, and camp experiences topped their list of booster rockets—you'll see them threaded through their comments:

- "After my best friend's 7-year-old brother died I realized the reality of death and heaven and wanted to live my life for Christ."
- "I was at a church camp and was really drawn to God. I had been pretty stagnant and decided to get 'more serious.' "
- "I went to Mexico and experienced what it was to truly serve and know God."
- "When I was about 15 I attended a youth conference and it kind of woke me up as to getting more serious about my faith. Letting my parents' faith that I grew up with my whole life become my own, so to speak."
- "During a missions trip I realized what an important part God was in my life and how I needed to trust him with my life. I knew I needed to make him the center of my life and the main influence."

3. Jesus-centered evangelism is primarily peer-to-peer.

Read between the lines of these students' comments and you'll see that their booster-rocket experiences created doubts and arm-wrestling matches with God. In fact, four out of five said they'd "really questioned" whether they were truly committed to Christ. And for most (54 percent) that time of great doubt came during their teenage years. Who helped them through those doubts to find their way back to Jesus? They most often said "friends," followed by "family members" and "youth pastors."

Rahn says: "After [completing] a two-year study of youth ministries that consistently, historically draw young people to Christ, I cast my vote for peer-to-peer strategies. My research team discovered a peer outreach strategy at the core of every evangelizing youth program we targeted. In every case, kids who were trained to reach other kids produced the most fruit with the smallest time investment."[4]

Rahn says he and his team found several common threads running through youth groups that seem to evangelize well, including:

- *Teenagers who effectively evangelize pray more often, invite more often, and tell others about Jesus more often.* The teenagers in Rahn's study really stood out—they reported getting together with others to pray for their friends *three, four,* or *five times a week.* In Philip Yancey's book *Prayer,* he describes prayer as a missional partnership with God—in prayer we saddle up and ride with him on his great mission to rescue his beloved children.[5] But prayer, for most of us, is a discipline at best. We work at it—even the language we use to describe prayer betrays our true feelings about it. It's a discipline we must muster and master to get God to do what we want him to do. But the Jesus-centered prayer the kids in Rahn's study practice is nothing like an arduous task—they don't pray only at certain times, with certain words, in certain places, and in a certain tone of voice. Instead, they *converse* with God about the people who are most important to them.

So, instead of modeling prayer as an expected discipline or task, fill your retreats with surprise "prayer pit stops" that challenge kids to listen to what God has to say about their friends, or stop in the middle of your talk or activity and have kids talk to God about someone who pops up in their consciousness as they're thinking about your theme.

In addition to prayer, Rahn adds: "The evangelistically effective kids in our study are more likely than an average Christian teenager to invite friends to places (large group meetings and small cell gatherings) and conversations (with adult Christians and themselves) where they're likely to hear the gospel...[And] kids who are effective evangelizers simply tell others the gospel story, and their own faith story, more frequently than their Christian peers. In baseball-ese, they hit more home runs because they're getting more at-bats." One senior higher from New Colony Baptist Church in Billerica, Massachusetts (an exemplary youth ministry), said, "To see other people who don't have Jesus in their life makes me strive to be more like Jesus so I can reach them."

- *Teenagers who effectively evangelize are coached well by adults.* Rahn's research team found that evangelistically effective youth groups share one crucial trait. They all

---

4 Rahn's research results come from studies conducted and later published in *Contagious Faith: Empowering Student Leadership in Youth Evangelism* by Dave Rahn and Terry Linhart (Loveland, CO: Group Publishing, 2000).

5 Insights from *Prayer: Does It Make Any Difference?* by Philip Yancey (Grand Rapids, MI: Zondervan, 2006).

recruit and train spiritually mature adults to meet weekly (or more often) with teenagers—in groups or one-on-one—to coach, encourage, pray, teach, and generally help them grow as Christ followers. When these meetings happen less frequently, kids' evangelistic impact drops.

I know this might sound overly "masculine" and everything, but the truth is Jesus embodied all that is great about great coaches, and then some. In his "High Priestly Prayer" (John 17), he tells God out loud that he accomplished everything he'd been given to do. But most of his prayer orbits a profound truth—"It will be better for them when I leave, so I'm going to leave." Why would Jesus be so excited to…leave? Well, the road to Emmaus demonstrated that, for at least two of his disciples, much of what Jesus tried to get across as their coach hadn't really "stuck" yet. They'd heard him, lived with him, and watched him, but they hadn't yet been transformed by him. There was one crucial step left in his coaching work—to move from an *outside* influence to an *inside* influence. And that's why the Holy Spirit is so necessary—the Spirit is an inside-job kind of coach. The Spirit makes it possible for us to move from knowing about Jesus to knowing Jesus. Our best coaching is often to shut up and give way to the Spirit. I love this little nugget from Dietrich Bonhoeffer in *Life Together*: "Spiritual love will speak to Christ about a brother more than to a brother about Christ."[6]

THE VIEW FROM THE DUST MITE

I think we can choose almost any single coming-to-Christ story and bore into it like a dust mite to find the bass line or drivetrain of evangelism. So let's use Greg Stier's story that opened this chapter as a case study.

1. Most of us come to Christ because we're drawn to a God who's bigger than we thought and a life that's bigger than we dreamed possible.

When Stier described the real Jesus to the surly teenager behind him at that restaurant, he effectively shoved the Trojan horse Jesus out of the room. Once that teenager heard about a God who was way bigger and better than he expected, he couldn't help himself—"Jesus is awesome!"

Stier says, "Teenagers need a much bigger 'yes!' to overwhelm all the little 'no's' floating around in their brains that keep them from learning to share their faith. 'No, I can't share my faith because I don't know what to say' or 'No, I don't even know how to bring up my faith in a conversation' or 'No, what if they ask me a question that I don't have the answer to?' "[7]

Jesus certainly evangelized his disciples by offering them a "bigger yes." Did you ever wonder why grown men in the middle of long-practiced careers would

---

6 Quote by Dietrich Bonhoeffer from his book *Life Together* (New York: Harper & Row, 1954), p. 36.

7 Greg Stier quoted in "The Idiot's Guide to Evangelism Training," from the July/August 2006 issue of Group Magazine.

literally drop everything and risk their livelihood to start following an obscure "prophet"? The answer, I think, is in "I will make you fishers of men."

One of the youth leaders at the round-table lunch I've mentioned earlier threw out this profound nugget: "My main focus of conversation with my kids' parents is: 'Is there anything I can do to help you give your kids a grander vision of their lives?' " I love that because it's so like Jesus.

The "bigger yes" that Jesus threw out there for potential followers was the same "bigger yes" that Elrond offered Aragorn—"Put aside the ranger—become who you were born to be." We can communicate to kids—"Put aside your small identity and step into your true identity as a child of the King. Let go of your puny dreams and pick up a great one, and join God in the greatest adventure ever, the redeeming of his beloved ones."

2. Most of us are drawn to Jesus by people who can talk about him naturally because they've practiced doing it.

Did you notice the artful way Stier spontaneously entered into conversation about Jesus with the teenager in line behind him? He can do that because he's practiced doing it. The best guitar players started by learning chords—the basic building blocks of music. Some guitar-playing Web sites promise to teach willing students to "play like Clapton" in 30 days. But online guitar teacher Danny Poole scoffs at those claims: "Eric Clapton didn't learn how to play like Eric Clapton in 30 days...What most people don't realize is that there are no quick fixes when it comes to playing the guitar, or any instrument." The more Clapton practiced, the better he sounded. Even today, critics of Clapton's more recent music accuse him of...not practicing enough.

We all have to practice the "bass line" of evangelism first before we can play jazz on the streets. Stier has translated those bass-line chords into an easy-to-remember "Gospel" acrostic:

- **G**od created us to be with him.
- **O**ur sin separates us from God.
- **S**ins cannot be removed by good deeds.
- **P**aying the price for sin, Jesus died and rose again.
- **E**veryone who trusts in him alone has eternal life.
- **L**ife that's eternal means we will be with Jesus forever.

He says: "What's true of playing the guitar is true of sharing Jesus. The gospel's chords are more than a creed [kids] memorize—they're more like the high points in a story that spans Genesis 1 to Revelation 22; a story that just happens to be true."

3. We'll struggle to teach kids how to evangelize until it becomes an everyday expectation—for them and for us.

As we encounter others in our everyday life, are we looking for open windows and cracked doors in their souls? Evangelism is merely a fruit of sharing our real life, and real beliefs, with others who are doing the same. That's exactly what Stier did with a teenager who looked anything but "open" to the gospel.

John DuBall, youth and family pastor at Rochester Covenant Church in Rochester, Minnesota (an exemplary youth ministry), says: "We have a lock-in every year where students will take cards to hand out to friends...This is not a fun overnight—that was dead a few years ago. The point is that your friends can hear in a clear and concise way that you are a follower of Jesus Christ, and why it's worth giving your life over to Jesus. We had 260 students come last year. This was not because of me; the students caught the vision for impacting their friends for eternity and they ran with it."

If you have a beeline-to-Jesus ministry, and your students know it, you'll create an expectation in them that Jesus will likely show up in everything you do. They'll not only carry that expectation with them into their everyday lives, they'll also invite their friends to youth group activities with the expectation they'll be introduced to Jesus somehow, someway. The beeline literally infects every community gathering in your ministry, including that crucible of growth, the small group.

Small Groups

(WITH AN INTRODUCTION BY JEANNE MAYO)

ELVIS HAS ENTERED THE BUILDING

The conversation stopped and everyone looked up when "Elvis" entered the room. Now for the rest of the story...

I'm not sure why we nicknamed him Elvis. Maybe it was because the teenager wore a black leather jacket and carried his old guitar around everywhere he went. But I am very sure why the conversation abruptly stopped the first night he showed up at one of our small groups. *Elvis stunk!*

Now, I know I'm supposed to say it more politely: "He had a slight problem with body odor." But a "slight problem" would not have frozen the room like he did. He smelled so badly that within five minutes one of the female small-group leaders stepped outside to stop her stomach from going into reverse gear. The guy's odor left most people in the room mentally running to take cover.

I'm sure you're wondering why one of the small-group leaders didn't politely ask Elvis to leave, take a shower, and come back on another evening. Good question. I guess it boiled down to a Holy Spirit moment. You see, the only thing more obvious than the guy's odor was his low, almost desperate lack of self-esteem. It seemed clear that he was so lonely and socially needy that he didn't even realize how serious his odor problem was. It also seemed clear that showing up at our small group was a scary, almost last-ditch effort on his part to try to make some friends.

Just before Elvis entered our lives, I'd talked about the importance of treating people with Christ's immutable sense of love and respect in one of our small-group leadership meetings. My mantra for the evening was: "Friendship is the paved highway that the Holy Spirit most often travels." Most of the teenagers attending our small groups are from upper-class, white-collar homes. So I took a few minutes to challenge them to extend authentic friendship to teenagers who might not dress or act like them. I even pulled out the Scripture passage on "entertaining angels unaware."

I'm not sure any of us every thought that Elvis was an angel. But he did give all of us a great chance to remind ourselves what small-group ministries are supposed to be all about—building a sense of family while helping each other to grow spiritually. So here's the beautiful part. By the conclusion of Elvis' first small-group meeting, one of our teenagers privately had the privilege to lead Elvis to the real King, Jesus Christ himself.

Months went by. Elvis became the small group's most consistent, wholehearted participant. Yes, daily showers became a regular part of his life. But so did a growing sense of security, friendship, and confidence. By the time Elvis graduated from high school that spring, a row of about 15 of us from his small group attended his graduation ceremony to cheer him on.

You see, Elvis' mom died when he was very young, and his dad spent most of his after-work hours at the bar. So as best as we could tell, we were Elvis' only family as he walked across the platform to get his high school diploma that day.

What am I trying to say? Just that Jesus-centered small-group ministry will look different for many of us. But one of the non-negotiables will be our willingness to look past each other's "stink" while we give each other time to slowly become the true "star" Jesus thinks we all are. After all, Elvis Presley isn't the only person who's looking for someone to "Love Me Tender."

—JEANNE MAYO
Longtime Youth Pastor and President of Youth Source

Did Jesus have an "Elvis" in his small group? Well, some of his "white collar" disciples might have objected to the smell those blue-collar fishermen brought with them. Of course, Jesus was the ultimate small-group leader. For proof, all you have to do is examine the evidence.

So let's see...one person in his small group sort of, you know, betrayed him and then committed suicide. Well, actually, every single person in his small group betrayed him. And his closest sidekick in the group (Simon Peter) basically denied he even knew Jesus when it counted the most. And even though he was the best teacher who ever lived, and he performed all these incredible miracles right in front of them, and he promised to "be with you always," and he knew just how to build a welcoming, committed family environment—the whole group of disciples sort of fell apart when Jesus went to the cross.

It's a good thing Jesus is a firm believer in the whole death-to-life principle. "I tell you the truth, unless a kernel of wheat falls to the ground and dies, it remains only a single seed. But if it dies, it produces many seeds" (John 12:24). That "dead" small group went through a resurrection as real as his own. You and I have been grafted into God's family as a direct result of their faithfulness to God and one another.

But three years of learning to love and serve together wasn't enough for these guys. Their "small group" was held together not by their close relationships, but by their mission. They needed something better—higher—than relationships as their goal.

If you asked most youth workers about the gold standard for ministry priorities, most would probably say "relational ministry." And they'd mean that emphasizing friendships and growing relationships—especially in small-group settings—is very important. In fact, the deeper the relationships experienced in small groups, the better the youth ministry.

I've had so many conversations with youth pastors about the importance of relational ministry that it probably deserves its own shorthand—RM, maybe. In the midst of every conversation, my little defense attorney is screaming, "Yes, but..." And the "yes, but" here is relational ministry is only a means, not an end.

There's plenty of research evidence that shows kids are having fun and building good relationships in youth groups, but the evidence also reveals a generation of teenagers who practice a "religion" described by *National Study of Youth and Religion* researcher Dr. Christian Smith as "moralistic, therapeutic deism."

- *Moralistic* means life is all about making right and wrong choices—the goal is to be a good person who exhibits good morals.
- *Therapeutic* means that God exists for our pleasure, not the other way around. Faith in God is important because God can help us get what we want in life.
- *Deism* means that God is essentially unknowable—he exists, he's a moral lawgiver and judge, and he sometimes gets involved in our lives, but we can't (and don't want to) really have an ongoing relationship with him.[1]

Obviously, this isn't the gospel of Jesus Christ. *Moralistic, therapeutic deism isn't even about Jesus Christ.* Somewhere along the way many of us have decided that relational ministry—often in the form of thriving small groups—is an end, not a means. And I think that's a breeding ground for moralistic, therapeutic deism. We can "gain the whole world" by helping kids build great relationships with each other and "lose our soul" by not running the beeline to Jesus through those great relationships. Not too long ago I asked the youth pastors who read a column I write for our YouthMinistry.com e-newsletter to respond to me if they resonated with this means-instead-of-an-end problem, and here's a sampling of their voices:

- "Well, the first and foremost goal of youth ministry is definitely a relationship—but it's a relationship between our kids and Christ," says Jenn Buccafurni, an Ohio youth minister. "Once that's established, then the relationship with each other and with adults will follow because Christ's love will abound in them and they will react with the love of Christ towards all individuals."

---

1 From the *National Study of Youth and Religion*, and an analysis of the study by Dr. Christian Smith and Melinda Lundquist Denton in *Soul Searching: The Religious and Spiritual Lives of American Teenagers* (New York: Oxford University Press, 2005).

- "Although I enjoy developing relationships with teens and having our leaders do the same, our ultimate goal is to make disciples of Christ who will in turn make disciples of Christ," says youth pastor Dawes Dunham of Pennsylvania. "We desire to see students come to faith in Christ, mature in their faith, and reach out to their peers with the gospel."
- "We are not running another Boys & Girls Club—we are a church youth ministry," says Brenda Seefeldt, a longtime youth leader in Virginia and founder of the FamilyBasedYouthMinistry.org Web site. "The goal of youth ministry is to teach about the Christian faith and to give teenagers a chance to understand that faith and accept it as the foundation for their lives. Today's busy teenagers include youth group in their schedules because they want to come to church and learn about faith in Christ. There are many other options out there for developing close relationships with peers and with adults. But they are choosing church to get that *and* to learn about faith. We best not fail in that expectation."

SHOOTING HIGHER

Of course, as a means or conduit for drawing kids into a close encounter with Jesus, nothing's better than relationships. And nothing's better at building "grafted into my true family" relationships than small groups. But, again, we have to be shrewd about what we're pursuing.

I was sitting in a meeting of church leaders listening to them talk about the problems the church was facing trying to plant and nurture healthy small groups—adult small groups were struggling with the same problems as the small groups for teenagers. Lots of problem-solving strategies were thrown onto the table—more structure, better ways of recruiting, capitalizing on shared interests, and so on.

As they spoke, I thought of the "small group" we'd been a part of over the summer—our Pursuit of Jesus class. Because of the off-putting way we advertised it in the bulletin, it started slow—some Sundays we had only six or 10 people there. By the end of the class a palpable and powerful sense of community had developed among the regulars—one person wrote us a note that summed up what many others had told us: "I felt as though I was on holy ground."

I realized, sitting there in that meeting, that even though we'd made many other mistakes in creating this pursuit, and had sometimes missed the mark with the risks we took, we'd consciously not built the class around shared "sidelight" interests, social connections, or *any* outward concern for community. In fact, the utter lack of attention to traditional community building was cause for some concern for my wife. Instead, we'd set the pursuit of Jesus *alone* as the focal point for our gatherings. As we grew more intimate with him, we grew more intimate with each other.

To paraphrase C. S. Lewis in his great book on relationships, *The Four Loves*, [2] when we gaze into each other's eyes, the depth of relationship that's possible for us is less than the depth that's possible when we first stand side by side and gaze into the eyes of Jesus. Close-knit community in small groups is a fruit, not the aim, of pursuing Jesus. They serve the aim of Jesus-centered living, not the lesser goal of closer relationships.

Now, this doesn't mean we completely ignore the basics of building close relationships in small groups. It simply means we're always, *always* thinking of the beeline to Jesus and proactively finding ways to connect whatever we do in our small groups to the center of all things.

IT'S A SMALL WORLD, AFTER ALL

It's hard to find a youth ministry that's not "sold" on small groups, exemplary or not. A few years ago I asked my friend Doug Fields—pastor to students at Saddleback Church, Group Magazine columnist, popular writer and speaker, and author of the Foreword to this book—what it was like to work at the "it" church of our generation. He smiled, shook his head, and then told me that almost every week he had youth pastors from all over the country asking to come hang out with him to glean the secrets of his success. Bad idea, he said, because Saddleback's "secret" to success—the engine for its growth and impact—is its small group ministry.

Idea-hungry visitors, he told me, would see a creative and engaging large-group gathering, but they'd quickly get bored following him around to his Taco Bell appointments. His volunteer small-group leaders were the rubber-meets-the-road ministry leaders at Saddleback.

And that makes perfect sense. Jesus influenced the crowds (and in many cases infuriated them), but he used his small group to bring deep, life-altering impact. Saddleback's example is just one more reminder that Jesus knew what he was doing. But the small-group environment is just that—an environment for ministry. Smallness alone doesn't produce fruit. But a small group that's beelined to Jesus in everything it does will produce lifelong fruit. That's what I discovered when I assembled a team to "diagnose" the problems in a nearby church youth group's small-group ministry—remember Jonny from Chapter 4?

Jonny was a longtime volunteer leader who led a home-based small group for the seniors in the youth group. We sent a camera crew to record two of his small-group meetings; then our team of six met several times to watch the videos and brainstorm solutions. Our team found the beeline missing in his group, and we unearthed several key strategic issues that would make it much more Jesus-centered:

- The group meets in a home, but the environment isn't as cozy, intimate, or welcoming as it could be. Jesus-centered small groups work hard to create a "true family" atmosphere.

---

2 Theme is from *The Four Loves* by C. S. Lewis (New York: Harvest Books, 1971).

- Jonny was great at establishing a rapport with his kids, but he needed to assert his leadership role more by knowing his goal for every gathering and preparing a game plan and structure for carrying it out. Remember, the reason why Jesus withdrew, often, from his responsibilities was to enjoy his intimate relationship with God—he always emerged from these alone times full of vision and purpose.
- I've already mentioned, earlier in Chapter 4, that Jonny's discussion questions needed a serious jump-start and a clear connection to Jesus.
- The group members would be more deeply influenced if Jonny found a way to capture kids' full attention. You'd be hard-pressed to find stories of bored, disengaged people hanging around Jesus. That's because Jesus used a teaching style that emphasized experience and story. Some loved him with a passion; some hated him with a passion. But he knew how to engage them, either way.

We came up with a makeover plan that we hoped would move the group past relationship building as a primary goal and toward an intimate encounter with Jesus instead. Jonny implemented our suggestions at his next group meeting, and we sent our camera crew back to record what happened.

1. Create a relaxed, warm, and welcoming environment for "true family."
Before our makeover, the lighting in the group's meeting place (the front living room in a home) was bright, the chairs were hard, there was no music playing as kids arrived or left, and there were no snacks served—not exactly a "true family" environment.

So we took Jonny and a couple of his kids out to a home store and bought inexpensive new throw pillows, candles, and lamps. Then we bought some easy-to-serve snacks and beverages. Back at the home, we pushed the chairs back and scattered the large throw pillows around the floor. We moved a low table into the center of the room and put the lit candles and snacks on it. We turned off the bright overhead lights and turned on our new, warmer lamps. We moved a boombox into the room, and we chose some background music to play as kids arrived and chatted.

The new setting created a more intimate, comfortable, and conversation-ready environment. The "after" video shows kids more relaxed, closer to each other, laughing more, and participating more—our subtle changes communicated a deeper sense of belonging.

2. The leader's job is to lead—small groups are a "benevolent monarchy."
Before the makeover, Jonny knew how to raise a topic for discussion but didn't have a good grasp on where to take it once it started—he sometimes communicated to the group that he didn't know where he was going. Jesus was a master of knowing

where he was going—he habitually transformed random conversations and encounters into the essential pursuit of his Father.

On the night of our makeover, the group was supposed to focus on the Sunday night theme—"Who is the real Jesus?" I asked Jonny to tell me what he hoped would happen that night. He said, "I want them to have a deeper understanding of Jesus." So to fuel a "here's where we're going" momentum, he and I agreed to make the goal of the evening this: "Lead kids into a deeper understanding of Jesus." I asked him to connect everything he did that night back to that goal like (again) spokes to a hub. In addition, I created an outline for the evening that included an icebreaker activity, reflection questions, a conversation-creating learning experience, engaging discussion questions, and an application challenge.

On the makeover night there was a different momentum, clarity, and direction to the discussion. The discussions were better, with every young person participating, because they sensed a clear plan for the evening. As kids deconstructed their mental models of Jesus and began encountering him as he really is, you could see the relational walls dropping.

3. Follow a Jesus-centered learning progression—experience, reflection, interpretation, and application.

In the pre-makeover meetings, Jonny's small group often meandered and skipped its way through a loosely defined discussion topic. Only a few young people participated in the discussion. If they decided to go on a rabbit trail, the whole group had to go with them. I asked Jonny to inject a targeted momentum to the evening by using a learning progression that's drawn from a WDJD mind-set.

It starts with an experience—as it so often did with Jesus. In this case, we had two experiences to work with. First, the previous Sunday night's large-group gathering was an experience the small group was supposed to debrief. In addition, I asked Jonny to add a new experience to the Tuesday evening gathering that connected back to the Sunday night theme. So first we help kids reflect on the experience, then we help them interpret a biblical truth that's connected to it, and then we help them apply that truth.

The night of our makeover, I asked Jonny to have his kids play an icebreaker game that reintroduced the theme of the night, followed by some reflection questions designed to get them thinking about what they remembered from the Sunday night gathering. Then the kids watched a simple PowerPoint slide show I created that showed 15 different ways our culture has depicted Jesus (I just googled for "images of Jesus" and got all I needed). As they watched the slide show, kids each quickly decided whether they thought each slide was a true or false depiction of Jesus. Then they got together with a partner to discuss the similarities and differences in their opinions.

To move into the "reflection" step, I had Jonny ask kids: "What did you learn about the way we see Jesus by watching this slide show? How does this slide show experience connect to the theme of Sunday night?"

To move into the "interpretation" step, I coached Jonny to say something like: "Our goal tonight is to deepen our understanding of who Jesus really is. Let's start by looking at a Scripture passage—it's John 14:1-10." After the Scripture reading, Jonny broke the group into trios to discuss my "Jesus—nice, fierce, or mysterious?" question. After 10 minutes of discussion, the group got back together to debrief.

Finally, for the "application" step, I asked Jonny to challenge kids to choose one of three ways to apply what they'd learned that night. For example: Look for an opportunity to do something in the spirit of Jesus, and then report back on what you did.

Because this progression introduced Jesus-y surprise and focus to the discussion, everyone was drawn into it. Kids were engaged in critical-thinking conversations that challenged, encouraged, and taught them something. And the gathering extended into their everyday life through the application challenge.

That night I saw what could happen if a small group's goal shifted from the lesser pursuit of relationships to the higher pursuit of Jesus. And, just as C. S. Lewis told us, you could see deeper relational possibilities unleashed in the group because they were drawing closer to Jesus. The trappings that surround a healthy group are like a well-built table—strong enough to set heaping platters of Jesus food on it.

Outreach

(WITH AN INTRODUCTION BY DAVE LIVERMORE)

GOD WITH SKIN

Here's something that sounds obvious—Jesus must be central to how we engage youth in service and mission. But what does that really mean? How is the service done by a Jesus-centered youth ministry different from service done by any group of teenagers?

In one sense, maybe there isn't a whole lot of difference. We should celebrate anytime young people truly engage in serving others. In fact, some of the greatest lessons I've learned about how to nurture service among youth have come from groups that are not explicitly Christian.

On the other hand, something ought to clearly set apart our service as Christ followers. At the heartbeat of Jesus-centered service is a proactive commitment to look at how Jesus himself served and engaged in mission.

To understand how Jesus served, we have to look at the backstory in the Old Testament. Particularly from Exodus onward, it's very clear that God's ears are tuned first and foremost to the cry of the oppressed. We see this most clearly when God rescued his people from the heavy hand of the Egyptian empire (Exodus 3 and following). In turn, God calls his people to do the same on his behalf with other nations by becoming a "kingdom of priests" (Exodus 19).

Though Israel does a less than stellar job in its "priestly" role, it's through Israel that Jesus comes on the scene. God himself shows up in the flesh to rescue all of humanity. And through Jesus, we get to see how God looks, thinks, acts, and serves. Essentially, we get to see God the Rescuer with skin on. Jesus becomes the living expression of the mission God had originally given to Israel.

Jesus says, "Repent, for the kingdom of heaven is near." It's like he's saying, "Turn and come back. There's a new kingdom on the scene. It's not another empire that exploits people so that the rich can become richer on the backs of the poor. Instead, it's a subversive kingdom that's oriented around bringing freedom. It's a kingdom that elevates the poor and the meek! Come join it!"

As Jesus is resurrected to the Father's right hand, the disciples are left to continue his mission of rescuing. Even though Jesus' earthly ministry is "over," God continues to wear his skin through the body of Christ—the church. He designed us to be his agents of redemption who rescue people personally and from systems of injustice.

So let's fast-forward a couple thousand years to 21st-century youth ministry. What's it look like for our youth ministries to continue to give people living experiences with the rescuing God? That's the key question for us to consider in thinking about Jesus-centered mission and service.

More and more youth ministries are incorporating acts of kindness and compassion as central to their service and missions projects. Some groups debate about whether the acts of kindness and service projects are merely a way to give people the "real" gospel or whether they're actually part of the gospel. If we are to learn anything from Jesus, it seems one without the other is an incomplete expression of his gospel. And to be honest, most of our brothers and sisters in the non-Western church are perplexed that we even waste time arguing about this. The gospel *must* be proclaimed and embodied.

Jesus' own service provides some much needed perspective on another area of debate as well. There's a tendency among many youth ministries to emphasize *personal* salvation and redemption while ignoring the broader issues of social justice; other youth ministries tend to do the opposite. Both expressions of mission are absolutely essential if we're going to be serious about Jesus-centered service. We need to simultaneously call our students to Billy Graham–like evangelism and Martin Luther King Jr.–style activism as we pursue Jesus-centered service and mission.

The more we spend time looking at Jesus, both personally and with our youth, the more compelled we will be to get up and extend the rescuing arm of God to the plight of those around us, near and far. Look around you. God has skin!

—DAVE LIVERMORE
Grand Rapids Theological Seminary and Intersect

D ave's take on Jesus-centered "activism" reminds me of a fascinating little research project I did for Group Magazine some years ago. I wondered what common threads we'd find if we studied some of the most "youth-friendly" churches in North America.[1] So I worked with two Group Magazine interns to contact denominational offices asking for recommendations of youth ministries we could explore. Then we took our list and started a phone-interview marathon.

One of the striking similarities we found was that every one of these church youth ministries had an obvious and passionate emphasis on outreach. Jim Burgen, youth pastor at Southeast Christian Church in Louisville, Kentucky, at the time of our interviews, said his group members led outreach clubs on high school campuses, did

---

1 From phone surveys conducted for the article "The Seven Signs of a Pro-Youth Church," in the March/April 1999 issue of Group Magazine.

volunteer work in Louisville's inner city, and headed work projects for senior citizens. The goal, he said, was "to be radically committed to God and to love one another unconditionally...We've got to keep our arms open wide."

Rick Janzen of Dalmeny Bible Church in Dalmeny, Saskatchewan, said his group was split 50/50 between churched and unchurched young people. He emphasized to his kids that outreach is a part of everyday life. "Some youth are overwhelmed," he said. "They can't believe it when they see that the church supports them. They can't believe people really care this much."

DID JESUS "CLOSE THE DEAL"?

Dave Livermore's "God with skin" metaphor is a great explanation for the necessity of serviced-minded outreach—"They can't believe people really care this much." Short-term missions and outreach projects communicate the heart of Jesus to those who don't know him. But the criticism often leveled at service-based outreach is that it rarely "closes the deal"—evangelistically speaking. The truth is, Jesus rarely "closed the deal" in his interactions with people. Think of the number of times Jesus healed people or cast out demons from them without saying a word about committing their lives to him. Often, the most he got was a "thank you" for what he'd given them.

Here's what happened when I searched for "Jesus healed" on www.BibleGateway .com—notice what Jesus says and does, and doesn't say and do, around each healing or demon ejection (of course, this is just a sampling of the search results):

- *Matthew 9:22—"Jesus turned and saw her. 'Take heart, daughter,' he said, 'your faith has healed you.' And the woman was healed from that moment."*
- *Matthew 12:22—"Then they brought him a demon-possessed man who was blind and mute, and Jesus healed him, so that he could both talk and see."*
- *Matthew 15:28—"Then Jesus answered, 'Woman, you have great faith! Your request is granted.' And her daughter was healed from that very hour."*
- *Mark 1:34—"And Jesus healed many who had various diseases. He also drove out many demons, but he would not let the demons speak because they knew who he was."*
- *Luke 9:42—"Even while the boy was coming, the demon threw him to the ground in a convulsion. But Jesus rebuked the evil spirit, healed the boy and gave him back to his father."*
- *John 5:13—"The man who was healed had no idea who it was, for Jesus had slipped away into the crowd that was there."*

Do you notice how Jesus healed people—cared for their most desperate, temporal needs—without the kind of "deal-closing" behavior we look for to "legitimize" service-oriented outreach? When we love people by helping them with no strings attached, we're moving in the spirit of Jesus.

Tina Hickey is a volunteer senior high youth leader in a suburban Seattle church. She e-mailed me to tell me about her group's 15-year tradition of road-tripping to a nearby town to put on a summer vacation Bible school for disadvantaged kids. The focal point of their outreach is to love poor children in tangible ways, and their long-term commitment to this service has created deep relational ties between the two communities.

Tina wrote to me: "I once read a definition of 'old-school' evangelism described as 'arrogant benevolence,' or the idea that we are nice to those who aren't as good as us to get them saved so they can be as good as us. Yuck! We chose to be deliberate in our 'relational' mission style because Jesus calls us to love others, and it turned out to be a major blessing in the lives of our entire team and our church...Our little kids talk about going on the mission trip for years, waiting for the summer after eighth grade to arrive. This is a natural way to begin teaching at an early age what it means to be a representative of Christ to those around you. As each new group of kids comes up to our high school group, the emphasis is for them to live as missionaries every day in their own community...They are challenged to find a way to be 'Jesus with skin on' to the world outside their door...That's what it means to be the body of Christ."

A HUNGER FOR SOMETHING BIG AND JESUS-LIKE

Woven through Tina's story is an undeniable truth—today's young people have a hunger to move in the spirit of Jesus. One teenager who's part of an exemplary youth ministry at Travis Avenue Baptist Church in Fort Worth, Texas, told an interviewer: "Service is being Christ-like and we are taught to live a Christ-like walk. It isn't how you achieve it—it is a result of it."

North American youth leaders have picked up on this hunger. Researchers with the *National Study of Youth and Religion* found that almost a third (29 percent) of all 13- to 17-year-olds in the United States have gone on a mission or religious service trip—that's an astonishing 5.5 million teenagers[2]. And I know that more than two-thirds of all Group Magazine readers say they're considering taking their group on a domestic outreach trip this year.[3]

The hunger kids have for outreach experiences is, in part, a hunger to do something really big with their lives. Look at the example of the 24-7 Prayer Movement. It started when a youth pastor in Britain couldn't get kids to show up for a little 30-minute prayer meeting, but when he challenged them to pray all day, every day for several months, kids came out of the woodwork to join in. Now there are 24-7 prayer "boiler rooms" all over the world, with thousands of teenagers praying around the clock for their friends, family, and communities.[4]

More than 30 years ago, Group Magazine's birth coincided with the birth of an outreach program that's now called Group Workcamps Foundation

---

2 From the *National Study of Youth and Religion*, taken from the study's Web site at www.youthandreligion.com.

3 From the demographic survey of Group Magazine subscribers, 2005.

4 Information from the 24-7 Prayer Movement Web site at www.24-7prayer.com.

(www.groupworkcamps.com). Not long ago our workcamps people got a letter from Dr. James Taylor, who'd taken some of his youth-group kids to one of our camps a quarter-century ago. He wrote: "In 1983 we took six of our youth on a Group Workcamp to Boone, North Carolina. It transformed their lives. Today, years later, all six are either in full-time ministry, youth ministry, or married to a minister, and one is a missionary. They still talk about how that one camp changed their lives forever."

Taylor's story illustrates what most youth leaders already know from experience—that service to others is not only Jesus-like, it's a big life changer.

JUMPING ON GOD'S BANDWAGON

While attending a Short-Term Missions (STM) Forum sponsored by the National Network of Youth Ministries, I was reminded to re-connect to the true engine that drives outreach. Forum participant Sherwood Lingenfelter, provost and professor of anthropology at Fuller Seminary, threw a bolt of truth into a heated discussion about the real value of short-term missions when he said the first question we should be asking is this: "What is God already doing, and how can we partner with him in doing it?"[5]

Now, Lingenfelter is speaking Jesus' language. Jesus said this to the Pharisees who were already seething at his outlandish proclamations of intimacy with his Father: "When you have lifted up the Son of Man, then you will know that I am the one I claim to be and that I do nothing on my own but speak just what the Father has taught me. The one who sent me is with me; he has not left me alone, for I always do what pleases him" (John 8:28-29).

Jesus humbled his own agenda in favor of supporting his Father's momentum and agenda—"I always do what pleases him." To do that he was always, always building bridges from truth to action—helping his disciples be doers, not just hearers. And we help teenagers cement their God-given mission in life when we move them into experiences where they can "test out" their true identity, where they can find an answer to the last big question—"Who do I say I am?"

One teenager involved in the exemplary youth ministry at Thornapple Evangelical Covenant Church in Grand Rapids, Michigan, wrote this note to her dad about her experience on an outreach trip to Washington, D.C.:

> Dear Dad,
> I have a story that I really think you'll like, so I hope you read this. This morning was the first morning at a mission site. I was chosen to go to the earliest site, 6:30 a.m., to Third Street Church. It is a food kitchen in the bottom of the church. We started out by talking to the homeless who were there waiting for food, then singing, and preparing

---

5 From notes taken at the Short-Term Missions Forum sponsored by the National Network of Youth and Religion, in January 2006.

breakfast while listening to a sermon…I was in charge of giving one drink to every person in line who wanted one, but we were limited on supplies. Whatever we poured out was whatever we had, and we had only enough to fill three trays. We had so many people in the shelter that we sadly had to close the doors and turn people away. I looked around the room and was really worried that we would not have enough juice for everyone…I prayed right away that God would provide at least one for every person in the mission. The line formed and everyone started to come through. I kept praying and trusting that God would provide. Then everyone was able to come up and get seconds, some even took thirds! We had plenty of juice for EVERYONE to have their fill and when we cleaned everything up and most everyone had left, I noticed I had ONE extra juice! I thought it was amazing how abundantly God provided and I felt like I had experienced a tiny bit of the feeding of the 5,000 with only a few loaves of bread and fish.

When this teenager was challenged to serve others as Jesus served, she not only discovered something about Jesus, she learned something about herself.

Again, the Apostle Peter is the perfect example of this. First, Jesus told him who he really is ("the Rock"), and then that name was tested. Peter betrayed Jesus by denying him. If Peter was anything like you and me, he likely was sure that his name was anything but "the Rock" during that time. But Jesus gave him the opportunity to re-embrace that name by entering into ministry—into his great outreach to the lost sheep of his Father.

In Peter's experience, and most likely in ours, "Who do I say I am?" is the toughest question to answer. Over the years as we try to answer it, God's enemy insinuates blatant lies masquerading as true answers. It takes a series of decisive moments—the kind kids often experience in the midst of an outreach—to significantly beat back those lies and embrace the truth.

I love the climactic scene in *Napoleon Dynamite*, when Napoleon realizes his friend Pedro is going to lose the election for school president because he's prepared no required "skit" for his presentation. So Napoleon, a loser on every scale ever concocted by teenage culture, decides to act. He gives what he has to give to serve his friend—it just happens to be the elaborate dance moves he's learned by watching an R&B "learn to dance" video. He pops in a cassette of the music he's practiced to so many times and wins over the crowd with not only his eye-popping moves but his sheer chutzpah.

Pedro wins the election, but Napoleon cements his identity—and it's not "loser."[6]

I think this one "payoff" scene well illustrates why *Napoleon Dynamite* was such a huge cult hit with teenagers. They're all longing to step into a crisis moment and cement their identity as a person who powerfully changes things for the better.

6 From the film *Napolean Dynamite*, released in 2004.

In practical terms, "as-we're-doing-it ministry" means scaring kids—in a good way. Jesus-centered outreach is all about asking them to do something scary: create something completely new (a worship service for the whole church?), serve in a setting that's far outside their comfort zone (a workcamp or missions trip?), or to reach out to people whose problems are beyond their ability to solve (not just feeding the homeless, but learning their stories?).

In short, our job is to ask them to get out of their "boat" and walk on water. This is what outreach is for—introducing managed crisis into kids' lives so Jesus can access their deeper places.

Several years ago I created a survey for Group designed to unlock the top reasons why Christian kids' faith in Christ has deepened and grown over the years—we asked more than 10,000 Christian young people to fill out the survey.[7] Their number one answer was "parents." Nothing helps a teenager grow in his or her relationship with Christ more powerfully than a parent (more on that later). Running close behind "parents" was the number two catalyst for spiritual growth: "a tragedy, crisis, or great struggle."

Not all crises are unplanned—we can actually introduce "controlled crises" into kids' lives for the purpose of helping them answer this crucial question—"Who do I say I am?" That's what outreach does. When Jesus sent his disciples out into the countryside in pairs to do what he'd been doing, he plunged them into an outreach adventure—a controlled crisis. I call these outreach adventures Planned Direct Crisis Experiences.

Planned Direct Crisis Experiences can include workcamps, mission trips, service projects, retreats, and wilderness adventures. A new environment, challenging responsibilities, new relationships, and lots of time—that's a great equation for plunging kids into a crisis so they can embrace who they really are. And it really "works."

Not long ago I was watching some of the raw video footage our workcamps people had shot to include in a promo video. One collection of interviews was targeted at the "personal outcomes" kids experienced through their participation in a workcamp. It was amazing to hear teenager after teenager say essentially the same thing about their experience—"I learned something about who I *really* am at this workcamp."

To loop back to Dave Livermore, when a teenager learns something about who he or she really is, that teenager is experiencing the deep joy of living as "Jesus with skin." And it's hard to find a youth ministry tool that's more suited to introducing kids to their Jesus identity than outreach.

---

7 These are results from a survey of more than 10,000 Christian teenagers attending Group workcamps in the summer of 2003.

Engaging Culture

(WITH AN INTRODUCTION BY WALT MUELLER)

THE REAL CULTURE WAR

If you could somehow look ahead 10, 20, or 30 years and see the shape your students' faith will take as they live their adult lives, what do you hope you'd see? I'm guessing you'd want to see a mature and growing faith. But what does that really look like? And what should you be doing now to prepare them for a lifetime of mature and growing faith? A good place to start is by choosing a side in the "culture war" and equipping your students to pursue Christian maturity by doing the same for the rest of their lives.

The "culture war" I'm talking about is not the one that's gotten the most press over the last few decades—that is, the culture war that's seen Christians rally the troops to fight societal problems and ideologies. Rather, it's the culture war that's been raging since Jesus ascended into heaven, the one being fought *inside* the walls of his church among those who call themselves his followers.

In his classic book *Christ and Culture*, H. Richard Niebuhr describes this "enduring problem" as the "many-sided debate about the relations of Christianity and civilization." To use battle language, the side you take in this war "within" shapes your approach to a level of effectiveness in your interactions with the world "without." One of the essential and most important lessons we can teach our kids is to come to an understanding of how to interact as Christ's followers with the world around them.

Throughout the course of church history and in our youth ministries today, we can see evidence of three distinct approaches to teaching and living out our relationship to culture. Which one should we be modeling and teaching to our teenagers?

When we take the approach of *accommodation*, we ignorantly or deliberately believe, and live out, cultural values and behaviors that are contrary to a biblical worldview. It's like we become the dog that's being pulled here and there wherever the culture on the other end of the leash chooses to lead us. This explains many of the recent research findings that point to few differences between the values, attitudes, and behaviors of Christians—young and old alike—and those who claim no allegiance to Christ at all. Failing to integrate faith into all of life, those who accommodate the culture profess allegiance to Christ but live no different than the world.

A more deliberate approach that's seen in many youth ministries today—perhaps yours—is *alienation*. With this approach, our homes and youth ministries become places where we seek to protect and defend ourselves and our children from the evil and offensive influence of culture by constructing "bunkers" in which to retreat and hide. To some degree, we conclude that non-Christian people, institutions, and cultural elements are hostile and dangerous to us and our faith, that we are to be separate from the world not only in attitude but in proximity, and that life is only about surviving and enduring our time on earth until Christ returns or we go to meet him in death.

Of course, I think the first two approaches to our relationship with culture are seriously flawed. A third approach, *engagement*, is the one modeled and commanded by the Christ who calls us to "come and follow me"...yes, right into the culture. This approach sees the culture as a mission field ripe for redemption. The place for Christ's followers—young and old alike—is to infiltrate the world, live in the culture, and thereby exert an influence that God uses to transform individuals and institutions.

Those who choose accommodation simply do as the world pleases.

Alienation leads people to escape into the supposed safety of their bunkers.

But engagement allows us to communicate God's agenda in the world as those of us who've been rescued by God live redemptively in the world he made and sent his son to redeem.

We are all—young and old alike—particular people who have been created by God to live in this particular time and place in culture and history. We are meant to be here, and while we're here we must live out the will of the Father that Jesus prayed the night before his death (John 17)—that while we no longer belong to the world, we are to continue living in the world. As we live in the world, our charge is to be the hands and feet of Jesus—his presence—carrying on his mission. The will of God is that our students *engage* the culture... both now and 30 years from now!

—WALT MUELLER
President of the Center for Parent/Youth Understanding

After Walt Mueller sent me his piece to kick-start this chapter, I wrote him this e-mail: "This is great—it's eerie how kindred I feel with your approach to all this. We even use some of the same language to describe the 'third' approach to responding to culture. I thank God for you."

And I really do. In today's church it's rare to find such an eloquent spokesperson for the "third way"—conventional Christian wisdom typically chooses either tacit accommodation or tacit alienation. Both of those paths essentially pivot around an Old Testament "us versus them" mind-set—we're either with them or against them, but rarely "with them to redeem them."

Every Bible comes equipped with a New Testament because a guy named Jesus arrived on the scene to fulfill—to redirect—the Old Testament system of holiness-through-separation. Jesus is already holy, and we're invited to share that holiness only as grafted-in brothers and sisters to him. Now, we don't need separation to be holy; in fact, Jesus asserts that his Father's mission of redemption *requires us to not be separate.*

BOUNCING OVER THE POTHOLES

But what does the "third way" of engagement really look like in a Jesus-centered youth ministry? There are lots of potholes in the proverbial road—and some could swallow a car.

Over Group's three-plus decades as the world's most-read youth ministry resource, our commitment to using mainstream music, films, video games, and newspaper articles as kick-starters to biblical and critical thinking has single-handedly filled up my psychological capacity for hate mail. But I'm guided by a passion to act on Jesus' challenge to be "in the world but not of it." For centuries the church has done a great job pursuing the back end of that challenge—we've so distanced ourselves from the world that we've earned distinction as a "Christian ghetto." In biblical terms, we're in serious danger of losing our "saltiness." Salt can't season itself—it must infiltrate something foreign to itself before it makes an impact.

Another "marker moment" in my leadership of Group came several years ago when I asked student leaders in youth groups across North America to journal what they saw, heard, spoke, and experienced on the very same day. These were cream-of-the-crop kids handpicked by their youth leaders, so I was a little stunned when the journals came back with few or no references to Christ's influence in their everyday lives. Curious, I gathered another diverse set of youth group kids and videotaped interviews with them. I wanted to know if they felt they could be "real" at church. The answer was a resounding "no."

But why? In effect, these kids told me they knew their cultural baggage would not be welcome in a church that had removed itself from culture. So they played the game, contorting their personalities to fit both the mainstream and Christian ghettos.

That ignited a fire in me that's still burning strong. Kids want a church that's unafraid to move in the culture because it's assured of God's primacy over it. That means our Jesus-centered imperative is to encourage conversations in kids' native tongue—popular music, popular film, popular TV shows, and popular gaming.

"In but not of" means we never embrace all the values represented in media influences and secular culture, but we faithfully use what kids are already attracted to in order to spur gospel-filtered discussions. A church that requires "outsiders" to speak its language first is a church that's unwittingly working hard to distance itself from those it's trying to reach.

Jesus never modeled or advocated distance in ministry. In fact, he so closely attached himself to "worldly" people and environments that some claimed he was "of the world" himself. By those standards, most youth ministries could use a little more worldliness.

The bottom line here is that if we think we're producing mature Christian young people by repeatedly damning popular music, contemporary books, and current movies and video games, we're confused. Hiding kids from the culture they live in, or blasting its most obviously pagan aspects, teaches them to fear it and distrust us. They either learn to adopt a "survival" mentality that honors rigid, powerless, self-centered living over impacting the world with the truth Jesus died defending, or they develop two alter egos so they can function in both the mainstream world and the church world.

A MAP OF ENGAGEMENT

How can we urge teenagers to take Jesus up on his promise to make them "fishers of men" when, at the same time, we tell them to stay away from the ocean? Here's my down-and-dirty map for teaching kids to engage their culture, not adopt it or deny it:

1. First, we wake up.

Early in the 19th century, a Hungarian doctor named Ignaz Philipp Semmelweis discovered, almost by accident, that if he washed his hands between procedures the percentage of patients who died after surgery dropped from 25 percent to almost nothing. But his hand-washing strategy was considered so ludicrous by the medical establishment that Semmelweis was fired from the hospital and later died at a young age, crazed with despair over the wholesale dismissal of his discovery. In his profile of Semmelweis, Dr. William C. Wood says, "I think there are...lessons to be learned from [his] life. The first is why there was such resistance to truth. People were too busy to investigate personally what he presented...The physicians of Semmelweis' day, with few exceptions, did not examine the facts firsthand."[1]

As youth workers our *first* responsibility is to engage in kids' media influences firsthand. We wouldn't let a teenager travel alone to Baghdad without their parents' permission (though 16-year-old American teenager Farris Hassan made the national news in late 2005 by doing just that), so why would we let them go to the Baghdad-like world of a video game like Grand Theft Auto without going there first or going there with them? First, we find out what kids are into, and then we go to www.imdb.com or www.comingsoon.net for movie trailers and information on current-release films, www.gamespot.com or www.gamerevolution.com to test-drive video games, www.amazon.com for track samples from albums, and we google their favorite TV shows to find fan sites and network home pages.

---

1 From a brief biographical paper "The Story of Ignaz Philipp Semmelweis" by William C. Wood, M.D.

2. Use what's common to teenagers, but use it shrewdly.

When Jesus used fishing, farming, money, or common cultural practices to unveil his good news (bad news to some), he was bridging God's transcendent truths into the everyday world of the people. But he was selective about the cultural practices he used as "bridges"—for example, he never used idol worship as a discussion starter.

My basic rule of thumb is this: If most teenagers have seen it, listened to it, or played it, then it's incumbent on us to consider using some part of it as a launching pad for an exploration of truth, as revealed by Jesus. The key word is "consider"—if you're worried about how profane a cultural influence might be, choose another widely experienced influence that's not as profane. But don't forget that Jesus chose to use some cultural practices (foot washing, picking wheat on the Sabbath, for example) that were highly offensive to the religious people of his day.

At Group, one way we've tried to move more deeply into Jesus' bridge-building calling has been to create an online resource called MinistryandMedia.com and a companion department in the magazine. Both offer background, critique, and biblical discussion questions for feature films, video clips, popular songs (both mainstream and Christian), video games, and breaking news (go to www.ministryandmedia.com to explore more). Of course, many youth leaders are finding their own media snippets to use as Jesus-centered discussion starters—it's just easier to use something that's the fruit of more than 10,000 hours of ongoing development.

3. Teach them to think critically about their cultural influences.

Not long ago I created a survey for Christian teenagers I nicknamed the "In-But-Not-Of" study.[2] Our aim was to discover how kids felt the church was training them to engage their culture in a Jesus-centered way. Among many other eye-opening findings, we discovered that just 17 percent of Christian teenagers say their participation in a church youth group has helped them "a lot" to think critically about films or videos (the stats were 18 percent for non-Christian music, 12 percent for TV shows, 8 percent for video games, and 14 percent for Web sites).

Jesus often challenged the people of his day to think critically about their cultural practices—for example, he prodded his disciples to consider who was making the bigger sacrifice, the rich religious leaders who made a lot of noise when they gave out of their excess income, or the widow who put a penny into the temple offering even though it was all she had (Mark 12:41-44).

I think we're Jesus-centered when we teach kids to critically "push back" against every cultural influence in their life. Here's an example of what I mean:

Plan and promote a video-gaming lock-in—have kids bring their systems and gather enough monitors to accommodate the crowd. Assert your right to screen and

---

2 Survey results are from a study conducted with more than 10,000 Christian teenagers attending a Group workcamp in the summer of 2004.

approve the games kids can bring to play. After a few hours of gaming, gather them for a snack and a little diving-board action. I mean, challenge kids to come up with a list of five things—positive or negative—that the game they were playing was teaching them. Then ask: If you had your own kids, which of these things would you want to teach them, and which ones would you not want to teach them? Explain. Then lead them in an exploration of Philippians 4:8 by pursuing what Jesus thought was "true...noble...right...pure...lovely...admirable...excellent...or praiseworthy."

4. Regularly force kids to solve problems that require critical thinking.

Find and give kids biblical problems to solve. For example, why did Jesus treat the Canaanite woman who was asking him for help in Matthew 15 so harshly? Or why, in John 7, did Jesus tell his brothers he wasn't yet going to attend a feast in Judea and then later go? The key to making this work is asking many, many follow-up questions after kids give their first answers. Think of yourself as a miner drilling deep into the earth because you're looking for gold. You really want that gold, so don't give up easily.

You can also challenge them with cultural problems ("Should gay people have the same rights as married people?") and relational problems ("How far would you go to 'love your enemies' as Jesus commanded?").

5. Use one of Jesus' favorite opening lines—"You have heard it said...but I say..."—all the time in your ministry.

Jesus often spurred people to think about their cultural assumptions by saying, "You have heard it said..." He'd proceed to restate a commonly accepted cultural "truth" ("You shall love your neighbor and hate your enemy") and then push back with a kingdom-of-God truth ("But I say to you, love your enemies and pray for those who persecute you").

We're moving in the spirit of Jesus when we teach kids to slow down and think—when we show them how to pinpoint the accepted "truths" in their media and marketing influences and compare them to kingdom-of-God truths. Whether it's a song, a film, an advertisement, or an article, teach them to answer (and then *always* ask) these simple questions:

1. What's the overall message, in one sentence?
2. What "truths" is it teaching?
3. What promises is it making?
4. Who's sending the message, and why?
5. Are these messages, truths, or promises that Jesus honors? Back up your answer.

You can use literally anything in popular culture to spur critical-thinking conversations with your teenagers. Soon, when kids are listening to their iPods or watching a movie with their friends or paging through their favorite magazines, they'll hear or see something that will flex their critical-thinking muscle—"Is this a Jesus truth or not?" When that happens, you'll have helped plant a Jesus-centered way of living life in them.

Can you imagine worshipping a Jesus who was frightened by his culture or who stood on a mountain and railed against the pagan idol-worshipping practices common in his "mainstream" society? Jesus saved his "rails" for hypocritical religious leaders, not his culture. That doesn't mean he approved of idol worship—his mission was to "draw all men to himself" so that idol worship would fade away from disinterest. It's a prime example of the "wheat and weeds" principle I covered in Chapter 6. The more we grow the "wheat" in teenagers, the less room in their "soil" for "weeds."

Counseling

(WITH AN INTRODUCTION BY CHAP CLARK)

ENTERING IN WITH JESUS

Sarah began with, "I have never told *anybody* about this…" She eventually got to: "You mean Jesus sees who I am and what I've done? If that's right, then he'd want nothing to do with me!"

In between, Sarah shared with me the long-buried story of a small child being repeatedly molested by a neighbor. Sarah had shoved aside shame, guilt, and pain for more than a decade. She'd tried to pretend that she could "handle it" and yet could never quite shake the feeling that she was a dirty, unlovable person. It wasn't until that day at camp when Sarah allowed me into her story that the depths of her anguish began to spill out.

As we talked, she slowly allowed the wonder of grace to seep into her soul. For the first time in her life, she began to trust that Jesus actually cared, and more importantly, could do something to bring healing to her shredded heart.

Sarah's story is unique, but only in its particulars. One of the major shifts that's taken place in youth ministry the last few years is that stories eerily similar to Sarah's are becoming more commonplace. The issue may not be sexual, although far more of our kids than we realize are victims of some form of sexual abuse. But almost every teenager is sheltering a hidden past or harrowing present that causes them deep pain. The amazing thing is that in youth ministry we remain so committed to getting kids to "come" and to "accept" Christ (a term, incidentally, that's not even in the Bible) that we don't do a very good job at communicating the good news that God *accepts them already*, brokenness and all.

As we represent Jesus Christ to students in youth ministry, our call is to follow him in how he approached, honored, and cared for those he longed to redeem.

In John 4 we're told that Jesus broke the law, at least the law of social convention, when he sat alone with a "Samaritan-gone-wild" woman at a lonely well. He had sent his disciples into town ostensibly to buy food, but from the context it appears that Jesus knew exactly what he had in mind as he approached the well.

Although the details are obscure at best, the way that Jesus engaged this lonely, outcast woman is astounding. First, he connected with her by initiating a relationship. The woman would certainly have minded her own business if Jesus hadn't broken in. But then he moves from connecting to honoring her by how he not only continued the conversation but deepened it. She wasn't a "ministry target"—his treatment of her demonstrated that he saw her as a precious daughter of his Father. As Jesus drew her into a real relationship by talking with her, he let her know that she mattered to him.

After Jesus had established a connection and then honored her with the gift of conversation, he entered her story. In the text this turn looks rather abrupt, but a careful read reveals that there had to be more to the encounter. When the time was right and trust had been established, Jesus invited himself into her world by asking a probing question. Her response makes it clear that the way he connected, honored, and eventually came alongside her story was a little frightening to her, but she nevertheless experienced a rare and welcome emotional embrace. As they talked, he then drew her into his story, the story of redemption.

This is what we do—Jesus-centered youth ministry means we are initiators, committed friends, and gentle counselors who, like Jesus, don't push. Rather, we're present, available, and on the lookout for the opportunity to care. Like Jesus, this means at our core we're committed to building a ministry that

- initiates and connects;
- honors in relationship;
- gently enters the stories of teenagers, and
- always points to the great healer, Jesus.

—CHAP CLARK
Fuller Theological Seminary Youthworker Journal

A few days after Hurricane Katrina devastated the Gulf Coast region in 2005, I was driving on a lonely Colorado road, searching for a radio station, when I heard some big-name Christian leaders talking about the "opportunities" open to Christians in the wake of the nightmarish storm. They hammered home the importance of pushing the U.S. government to offer greater support for faith-based organizations and criticized Planned Parenthood for showing up at the Superdome to pass out condoms.

Meanwhile, the poor of New Orleans were literally begging for someone to rescue them from three killers—a hurricane, a flood, and roving bands of thugs. I had to turn the radio off—the Christian leaders' comments made my stomach knot up. I had no patience for "opportunity" talk.

Now don't get me wrong. As I mentioned earlier, crises do create "opportunities"—God can use them to pry open our tight windows and doors so he can get at our core. But in my mind, those Christian leaders I'd heard on the radio had totally missed Jesus' clear priorities. At the top, he's primarily concerned with entering into the sorrow, confusion, and fear of those who are desperate, grieving, and hurting.

ENTERING INTO THE LAND OF THE "OUTIES"

There are two ways to respond to crises in the lives of teenagers. We can subtly stand outside their stories, tossing them the equivalent of fortune cookies that have scriptural principles and prerogatives inside. Or we can passionately enter into their stories as Chap Clark suggests.

That's exactly what I experienced as I read my friend Allen Jackson's post-Katrina blog entries—Jackson is a professor of youth ministry at New Orleans Baptist Theological Seminary, and his school and home were swamped by flood waters, destroying many treasured personal items and forcing a temporary sojourn away from his wife and one of his children. Here's part of Jackson's blog entry for September 15, just 17 days after the devastating hurricane hit New Orleans:

Our culture is famous for "innies" and "outies." Back in doctoral work, I remember reading a book by Ralph Keyes entitled *Is There Life After High School?* which distinguished between the students who are part of the group and those who, for whatever reason, are left out. Our kids move in groups, tribes, and teams; and if you observe closely, everyone seems to settle in to their place in the food chain.

I am thinking about the effects of such a major disaster on individual teenagers and where and how they "fit in." I have two teenagers who had their worlds changed dramatically when we loaded up the car for what we thought was a few days away from our house until the hurricane passed. When the city went underwater, and the access roads were destroyed, and the martial law and mandatory evacuation orders stretched into weeks if not months, the prospect of returning to find those worlds intact became remote. Now they are in a new school, in temporary housing, a new youth group, a new town—a new world. Their place on the sports team and the drama team is no longer secure as they are "outsiders" to the system.

It has made me think again of how transitional many of our students are. They live in multiple homes, shared custody situations, sometimes moving to different living arrangements with unfortunate regularity. They have their world rocked by trials other than hurricanes, and for them it is simply a way of life. I am hurting anew for students who don't have stable homes or youth groups or adult support. They are consistently "outsiders" to the system.

What can we do? Jesus had much to say about those who were "in" the system and allowed others to remain "out." He understood the damage that can be done to someone's potential when their plans and dreams are short-circuited...Teenagers are remarkably shortsighted and present-centered. Hope is easily crushed when the current plan, team, club, activity, or relationship is suddenly ended.

Join me in being even more observant for those who are "outsiders" to our system.[1]

Allen is talking about entering into the loneliness and grief teenagers everywhere experience every day. Kids are longing for people to offer tangible love to them—that's both our opportunity and our mission.

CRISIS, THE GREAT DOOR OPENER

Metaphorically speaking, Christ-like presence in the midst of crisis means "diving into the deep end" of life with kids. In Chapter 7 I mentioned a study I conducted a few years ago—nine out of 10 Christian college students we surveyed said they'd had a crucial recommitment experience that was as significant as their conversion. Two-thirds of these students said the recommitment experience happened when they were teenagers and was fueled by one of four catalysts, including crises.

In Chapter 9 I explored how "planned crises" can help teenagers cement their Jesus-given identity. But unplanned crises—such as Katrina or parents divorcing or a friend's rejection or a sports injury or a deadly car accident that takes a friend—have an unmatched power to open a teenager to deeper healing. That's because they—and all of us—keep the door to our soul shut pretty tightly as a rule. Crisis cracks it open.

The key? When the crisis hits, is there a passionate Christian engaged in the student's life—not to answer unanswerable questions, but to peek through the cracked door? The right question for us at this point is: *Where* would Jesus be?" And the answer is: Right there in the middle of the crisis.

Adrian McMullen, the senior high community outreach director at First Presbyterian Church in Fort Dodge, Iowa (an exemplary youth ministry), says: "I learned a phrase: 'the intimate proclamation of the gospel.'...In those situations where a kid is in trouble or some vulnerability is exposed, 'you have the opportunity to present Christ to them in healing.' "

When an awake, engaged, Jesus-loving, and Jesus-centered adult enters into a teenager's crisis with determination, passion, and a purpose, that person becomes a partner with God in his greatest work—he or she takes what Satan meant for evil and uses it for good. We call that "counseling teenagers," but really we are simply living out Jesus' care and concern for each and every person in our group; we are letting a Jesus-centered lifestyle show itself in Jesus-centered counseling and ministry to a younger brother or sister in Christ.

Remember what Jesus did when his friend Lazarus was dead and buried in a tomb? Here's most of the story, taken from John 11—read it carefully, looking hard for what Jesus says and does in this situation:

---

1 Excerpted from a blog written by Professor Allen Jackson on the Web site for the Center for Parent/Youth Understanding, at www.cpyu.org.

On his arrival, Jesus found that Lazarus had already been in the tomb for four days. Bethany was less than two miles from Jerusalem, and many Jews had come to Martha and Mary to comfort them in the loss of their brother. When Martha heard that Jesus was coming, she went out to meet him, but Mary stayed at home.

"Lord," Martha said to Jesus, "if you had been here, my brother would not have died. But I know that even now God will give you whatever you ask." Jesus said to her, "Your brother will rise again." Martha answered, "I know he will rise again in the resurrection at the last day." Jesus said to her, "I am the resurrection and the life. He who believes in me will live, even though he dies; and whoever lives and believes in me will never die. Do you believe this?" "Yes, Lord," she told him, "I believe that you are the Christ, the Son of God, who was to come into the world."

And after she had said this, she went back and called her sister Mary aside. "The Teacher is here," she said, "and is asking for you." When Mary heard this, she got up quickly and went to him. Now Jesus had not yet entered the village, but was still at the place where Martha had met him. When the Jews who had been with Mary in the house, comforting her, noticed how quickly she got up and went out, they followed her, supposing she was going to the tomb to mourn there.

When Mary reached the place where Jesus was and saw him, she fell at his feet and said, "Lord, if you had been here, my brother would not have died." When Jesus saw her weeping, and the Jews who had come along with her also weeping, he was deeply moved in spirit and troubled. "Where have you laid him?" he asked. "Come and see, Lord," they replied.

Jesus wept.

Then the Jews said, "See how he loved him!"

But some of them said, "Could not he who opened the eyes of the blind man have kept this man from dying?" Jesus, once more deeply moved, came to the tomb. It was a cave with a stone laid across the entrance. "Take away the stone," he said.

"But, Lord," said Martha, the sister of the dead man, "by this time there is a bad odor, for he has been there four days." Then Jesus said, "Did I not tell you that if you believed, you would see the glory of God?" So they took away the stone. Then Jesus looked up and said, "Father, I thank you that you have heard me. I knew that you always hear me, but I said this for the benefit of the people standing here, that they may believe that you sent me."

When he had said this, Jesus called in a loud voice, "Lazarus, come out!" The dead man came out, his hands and feet wrapped with strips of linen, and a cloth around his face. Jesus said to them, "Take off the grave clothes and let him go."

GOING INTO THE CAVE

What are some things Jesus did to enter into this crisis? And what does his example teach us about entering into our kids' crises? Here's what I see from the story of Lazarus above:

1. Deeply moved, troubled, and weeping—that's what should come through the door of opportunity when a crisis opens it.

Our purpose in entering into a young person's crisis is to weep with them, to remind them of who God is, and to remind them of who they really are. Nothing is more powerful to teenagers than an adult who will weep on their behalf. Our sincere tears communicate passionate presence. But teenagers have learned the hard way to not let others see their treasure—especially the ways their treasure has been stolen, smeared, and defiled. Passionate presence says, "I see that treasure you have there—I appreciate and respect it for what it is."

One way to communicate passionate presence is to do what I call "asking the next question." It simply means training yourself to keep asking questions until you get a "real" answer. People almost always give up on a line of questioning before they get to breakthrough with it. Relax about awkward silence, wait, or ask the question in another way. Few teenagers will simply haul out their treasure and let you examine it, but most will throw out little clues to let you know where it is and what it is. Think of yourself as a detective trying to unravel a mystery—and the mystery is the young person in front of you. So keep asking follow-up questions until you get close to the treasure room—and remember to walk toward it with gentle determination and respect.

On my way to a youth conference at a college in a remote Canadian city, I rode in a van for an hour next to a 17-year-old student named Trevor. I spent about 40 minutes of that hour asking Trevor "next questions."

When I asked him why he traveled so far to attend the event, he told me he used to go to the Christian high school that's attached to the college and was looking forward to seeing his friends again. He left school before finishing his final year because he had an "incredible" job opportunity in the oil industry. No, he had no regrets about leaving early because he was making "really good money."

Something about his story didn't ring true to me, so I pursued possible alternatives to the reason he gave me for leaving school. He told me he didn't get along well with his parents. When I asked why, he thought for a while and then said, "They just have different morals than me." So I asked, "Are your morals better or worse than theirs?" He then described his parents as ultraconservative Christians who were unrealistic and inflexible.

I zeroed in on the blank spots in his story—he missed his friends at school and had a strained relationship with his parents, and now he was living hundreds of miles away on his own. The key to understanding Trevor, I thought, was unlocking the real emotions behind his decision to leave school. So I asked him what his "incredible" job involved. Basically, he spent his day measuring fuel in tanks and selling knickknacks at a commercial fuel outpost.

This was an intelligent, ambitious kid, and the details of his job didn't match his enthusiasm for it. But he was determined to make me believe he was happy because to admit his unhappiness would mean showing his tarnished treasure.

I discovered that Trevor lived in an apartment with his older brother, who was seriously disabled by a "mystery ailment." As a result, his brother—who'd once loved God—now hated him. I could see Trevor was desperate to be reminded of God's goodness, and he was longing for the Christian fellowship and environment he once took for granted.

There was nothing particularly outlandish or attention-getting about Trevor, and that made unlocking his soul even more difficult. Kids who dye their hair purple or wear black trench coats to youth group are exposing their souls for all to see. Kids like Trevor—commonplace kids—hide their souls in the familiar, like a diamond among rhinestones.

As the van pulled up to my little hotel, this is what I'd found in his "treasure chest": He never wanted to leave school in the first place, he desperately missed his friends and his God, and he traveled halfway across Canada hoping to find hope in God again. Because I repeatedly asked "the next question" with Trevor, he let me see some of his treasure.

2. The core that fuels our movement toward troubled kids is a determination to witness to the glory of God.

Here's an irony—at a time when more and more people are disconnected from each other, the number of celebrity magazines is climbing. Our curiosity is misplaced—while we feed our fascination for celebrity minutiae we largely ignore the riveting stories of "average" people. Of course, we're drawn to powerful stories, but we don't always recognize them in the everyday people surrounding us. We've lost our amazement, even though the greatest screenwriter who ever lived is writing those stories—God. And we celebrate the life stories we see in the Bible, but forget that he's writing *every person's* story, not just David's, Solomon's, or Paul's.

Because God is writing *every* teenager's story—creating beauty out of ugliness whenever it's offered to him—we unlock his glory when we unlock a teenager's story. Jesus-centered counseling moves toward kids with unrelenting curiosity because, like Jesus, our primary purpose is to bring more glory to God. And the glory of God is the release into freedom of his beloved children.

3. We risk what is most scary to us by "going into the cave" after young people.

In *The Return of the King*, the last installment of the *Lord of the Rings* trilogy, just after the scene I've already described in Chapter 6, Aragorn takes Elrond's advice and saddles his horse for a trip down the Dimholt Road to visit an army of dead people who "live" under a mountain. His mission is to give them a chance to repent for betraying a previous king of Gondor by joining his army in the war against Sauron. The elf Legolas and the dwarf Gimli insist on going with Aragorn. They arrive at the dark entrance to the mountain, having ridden through a spooky, silent valley. I'll let the script pick it up from there:

(*Before them, at the root of the mountain, is a sheer wall of rock towers...*)
Gimli: (*In a terrified whisper*) The very warmth of my blood seems

stolen away. (*Within the walls, a creepy dark door gapes like a mouth of night. Signs and figures are carved above its wide arch.*)

Legolas: (*Translating*) The way is shut. It was made by those who are dead, and the dead keep it. The way is shut. (*At that moment, a chill wind seems to rush out of the doorway. Aragorn stares into the blackness, his hair blowing wildly. The horses rear and buck in terror, turning and galloping away.*)

Aragorn: Brego! (*The three horses disappear. Aragorn turns resolutely towards the doorway. Then he says, with steely resolve...*) I do not fear death...(*Aragorn walks into the blackness. Legolas quickly follows...swallowed by the darkness.*)

Gimli: (*He's left alone. He hesitates, struggling with his fear.*) Well, this is a thing unheard of...An elf will go underground when a dwarf dare not. (*Gritting his teeth*) Oh! I'd never hear the end of it! (*Gimli plunges into the tunnel behind the others!*)[2]

When I show this scene to youth pastors, I ask them this question: "How is this scene a metaphor for passionately pursuing young people?" Usually, they answer that it's a perfect illustration of what it feels like to counsel broken, hurting, angry teenagers—the dark places in their souls seem scary because they use fear, anger, sullenness, and even abuse as guardians, keeping further hurt away from what's been damaged.

To go into the cave with young people means to bring light into darkness, to help them redirect the energy it takes to hide into pursuing God and participating in his great mission. This is what it means to bring freedom—not just to the person, but to those who need what that person has been given by God.

I love what Steve Merritt, longtime "Personal Growth" columnist for Group, says about "going into the cave" after kids. Merritt has been a counselor who specializes in working with teenagers for years. He says: "As a counselor I meet with cynical, skeptical, scared, and hurt teenagers every day, and each one asks the same three questions: 1. Do you understand me? 2. Are you going to be real, or are you like the rest of the imposters in the world? 3. Do you care?"[3]

You'll answer the first question for kids when you ask the right "next questions"—just the mere practice of asking kids "next questions" creates a powerful sense that you "get them." Merritt says, "Do you get what is stressing them out, what their fears are, what the unspoken terrain is just beneath the surface? God has to incarnate himself into their world through you (or your staff) before they're going to pick up a wooden beam and follow anybody anywhere."

You'll answer the second question when kids sense you're no longer posturing or game playing with them. I've mentioned tears earlier in this chapter—there's

---

2 From the shooting script for *The Lord of the Rings: The Return of the King*, by Fran Walsh, Philippa Boyens, and Peter Jackson, based on the book by J. R. R. Tolkien.

3 From Steve Merritt's "Personal Growth" column in Group Magazine, the November/ December 2006 issue.

no quicker way for kids to access your soul than through your sincere tears. I remember, during the crisis time with my wife 10 years ago, that she told me she wished she could get at the "real Rick" buried underneath my posing. For the first time I allowed my dammed tears to break loose—not because I felt sorry for myself, but because I *felt* my wife's sadness over what I'd withheld from her. Through the portal of my tears she *saw me* more deeply. Do you allow yourself to not just understand your kids but *feel* them? When you do, and they see your tears, they'll have a little portal into the real you (of course, they can also see you through your honest laughter, your own vulnerability, and by your riveted responses to them—but tears are still the most direct path to the soul).

The answer to the third question is locked up in a scene from the film *The Horse Whisperer* that I often show to youth leaders. In the film a cowboy named Tom Booker, who's renowned for his ability to rehabilitate physically and psychologically damaged horses, is just starting to work with a horse named Pilgrim, who was hit by a lumber truck while on a casual ride with his teenage owner. Pilgrim has recovered physically, but no one can ride him because his soul and spirit are so wounded from the accident.

During Booker's initial work with Pilgrim, the horse knocks him down and bolts into a wide Montana pasture. Booker wordlessly follows the horse into the pasture, where he kneels in the long grass and waits—the whole day and into the twilight, staring gently at the horse. As darkness creeps across the field, the horse has been convinced. He slowly ambles toward Tom, finally allowing him to stroke his nose and walk him back to the ranch.[4]

That's a perfect picture of what wounded kids are looking for: persistent, focused attention that proves we care.

4. We're not afraid of strong emotions, even when they're directed at us.

In Chapter 6 I drilled into the results of a survey I nicknamed "The Cool Youth Leader" study. Almost three-quarters of the teenagers who responded (71 percent) said they want a leader who "can handle my doubts, struggles, and strong emotions."

In the Lazarus story, when Mary finally left her home and ran to meet Jesus after her brother had already been dead for four days, she doesn't hold back her grief (and maybe a little anger)—"If you had been here, my brother would not have died." But Jesus sees past Mary's outburst to her hurting heart and reassures her that life is on the way.

5. Our ultimate goal is to partner with God to bring life where there is death.

When a youth group student suddenly died, the kids and adult staffers at First United Methodist Church in Valparaiso, Indiana (an exemplary youth ministry), were plunged into grief. Tammy Clark, youth minister at the church, told an

---

4 From *The Horse Whisperer*, released in 1998.

interviewer: "All of us to various degrees are (and have been) grieving. I say that initially because I don't want to give the impression that we've just sort of gone on...We believe in resurrection and on we go, but, although we are grieving, we are doing so as people with hope."

As part of its grieving process, the congregation created a prayer labyrinth in part of a new memorial garden—it was designed to offer solace for those who are struggling with sorrow. "We were supposed to have a lock-in that weekend [of the student's death], and instead we just sat and talked," said one teenager at the church. "That's the most youth I've ever seen at any youth meeting," said another. "We've all been there for each other," said another. "When someone has a problem, you can sit down and talk with them." Clark added that the relationships between adults and young people at the church are about "presence and companionship, rather than recruitment."

And it just so happens that "presence and companionship" are the twin forces of Jesus-centered counseling.

Volunteers

(WITH AN INTRODUCTION BY KURT JOHNSON
AND KATIE EDWARDS)

THE THREE E'S

When you think about it, Jesus was the first person in the church to develop a team of volunteers to help him fulfill his ministry call. Jesus had lots to do and a short time to do it. For three years, Jesus and his ragtag group of disciples forged a unique team that changed the world.

We've partnered in youth ministry together for 10 years—10 years of summer camps, surf outings, mission trips, and memories. We've learned a *whole* lot of youth ministry lessons, but one that we've been reminded about over and over again is that youth ministry really couldn't happen without a team of adult volunteers.

It's interesting that one of the first things Jesus did when he began his public ministry was to begin building a team to help out. But not *just* to help out: Jesus was building a team that would make an eternal difference.

Youth ministry is a fast-paced, stress-filled, never-ending job. It's tempting to focus on the various tasks at hand (planning the next event, writing the next lesson, T.P.-ing the next house...) and overlook the most important task: building a team to help make an eternal difference.

It makes sense that a Jesus-centered youth ministry would have a Jesus-centered approach to building a team. Let's take a quick look at three ways Jesus built his team and how we can learn from his example.

1. Jesus enlisted. Jesus didn't sit around and hope that what he was about to do would attract people to his cause. Instead, he proactively enlisted others to join his team. He made "the ask," and he made it in a compelling way. When he said to Peter and Andrew as they were casting their nets, "Come, follow me, and I will make you fishers of men," imagine how compelling that must have sounded to two young men who made their living being fishers of fish! Youth ministry is important stuff—important, exciting stuff!

Which is a more compelling attempt to enlist the help of others: "We have a group of ADHD seventh-grade boys, and we're desperate for someone willing to put up with them," or "We have an energetic group of seventh-grade boys and we've been praying for an enthusiastic leader—we think you may be it!"? Jesus enlisted others with a compelling message.

2. Jesus equipped. Jesus was a master trainer. He knew the stakes were high. In just a few years, his little team of fishermen, doctors, and doubters would have to continue his work. So instead of spending time lecturing them with fill-in-the-blank training sessions, he equipped them by giving them a whole lot of on-the-job training.

They messed up, asked tons of stupid questions, bickered and positioned with each other…but all the while they were being equipped with the tools they needed. For sure, there's a place in youth ministry to formally train and equip our leaders, but Jesus modeled that the best way to equip his team was to let them be a part of the action…to follow him around and do what he was doing.

3. Jesus empowered. Eventually, Jesus' disciples would need to be ready to launch out on their own, without his physical presence there to lend a hand. As he equipped them, he also began to empower them in little ways…as if to give them baby steps or little confidence boosters. He encouraged Peter's bold proclamation by encouraging him to walk on water! When the disciples shared their concern that the multitudes listening to him teach were getting hungry, he said, "You find them something to eat." Before he ascended into heaven, he empowered them with the Holy Spirit and reminded them of the task at hand.

Jesus, God in the flesh, chose to partner with those who loved him to expand his Father's kingdom—he enlisted, equipped, and empowered others to play a crucial role in his redemptive mission. He certainly *could* have done it all on his own, but because relationship is paramount to him, he decided to partner with…us. We've learned lots of lessons over the years. But the ones we learn from Jesus are the ones that matter most.

—KURT JOHNSTON
Saddleback Church, Orange County, California, Simply Junior High Ministry
—KATIE EDWARDS
Saddleback Church, Orange County, California

A few weeks ago I was meeting with my friend Doug Ashley, the middle school family minister at my church. I was telling him about this book thing I was working on—*Jesus-Centered Youth Ministry*. It was early fall, and he was giving me an update on how his volunteer recruiting had gone over the summer. He was excited by the possibilities some fresh faces represented.

Then I asked, "Is there anything Jesus-centered about the way you recruit and train your volunteer leaders?"

He thought for a moment—I could see those gears turning, because you don't want to say "no" to a question like that, do you? But he did say "no," at least at first. He told me he was a little embarrassed to describe to me how he recruits all his adult leaders. I just sat there and stared at him, with an expectant look on my face (at least, that's the look my brain was going for).

Then he said something accidentally profound: "Really, I look for people I'd like to hang around with for a long time and then I ask them to join me in ministry. My primary concern isn't whether they're young or really good with teenagers...the most important thing to me is how much I enjoy someone. I've surrounded myself with people I enjoy, expecting them to stick around with me for a long time."

A big smile crept up my face. I asked, "Well, how do you get them to stick around for a long time?"

Then a big smile crept up his face. He said: "I don't 'get them' to stick around. If they enjoy their relationship with me and with the other leaders, they just do—they become my volunteer team. If they don't enjoy me or the other leaders, they leave. The people who don't leave become my volunteer leaders."

Then I leaned across the table and said, with energy: "Well, you just described what I think was Jesus' approach to volunteer recruiting! He traveled the coastlines and marketplaces, inviting people whom he thought he'd enjoy to follow him. The people who stuck with him became his disciples—his 'volunteer team.' The people who didn't stick around became anonymous 'left behind' people."

As I was saying all this, Doug was nodding his head in agreement—probably quite happy that we'd decided his volunteer recruiting method was, indeed, Jesus-centered. Then I asked, "What do you think you enjoy about the people you enjoy?" He quickly replied, "I enjoy how much they're passionate about Jesus—that's what draws me to them."

RIDICULOUS RECRUITING

Of course this is how you'd recruit volunteers in the spirit of Jesus. But here's the funny thing about how Christ gathered the leaders who'd later plant his church all over the world—his "strategy" seems uncomfortably random and understated and almost accidental. In fact, it borders on the ridiculous:

"Hey, you there! That's right, the strapping guy in the front of the boat. I know you've given your whole life to working in the fishing industry. I know you have a family to feed and all, and I know you're right now in the middle of your workday and that your dad (who needs you to run the family business) is standing right behind you listening to this—but I was wondering if you'd drop everything, right now, and come follow me where I'm going. I'll teach you how to catch men as well as you've caught fish" (Matthew 4:18-20).

I think the first thing I would've said in response to Jesus if I'd been Simon Peter would've been, "Umm...I didn't catch your name..." Can you imagine yourself—or anyone you know—simply dropping his or her life at a random moment in favor of following after an obscure prophet who'd not even made a name for himself yet?

You're a better person than I am if you say "yes"—or you're possibly insane or a fifth-year senior at college. We have the barest of clues in Jesus' "fishers of men" comment. The driving force of every middle-aged man I know is to make sure his life is making the kind of impact he hoped for. It's as if you reach your mid-40s and realize you have less life to go than you've already covered, like the middle of the third quarter in a football game, and you'd better start "scoring some points" here or you might just lose this contest.

So maybe that was it.

Or maybe our conventional default answer resolves the dissonance for us—it worked because he's Jesus and we're not. I've always thought that was a cop-out, though. I think the truth is that Jesus could sense the hungry people—the people who had a latent desperation for God and were already standing with their toes over the cliff, ready to jump at something big and great and transcendent. I think Jesus' insights into the private hopes, longings, and fears of people have a lot to do with how passionately he paid attention to them...oh, and he apparently had that omniscience thing working for him, too.

Or maybe we don't really understand what it was like to live in Jesus' time, when a really good day was simply earning enough or growing enough to scrape by and survive. We live in the most affluent culture in the history of the world, and that means we'd have a lot to lose if someone asked us to leave all our stuff behind and just up and follow some guy who promised us a big adventure. We wouldn't do it any more than the rich young ruler would do it—he had too much on the line, too little desperation, to do what Jesus' other disciples had done.

I find it attractive and inviting and inspiring that Jesus' disciples were likely some of the most desperate people around. Maybe some of them were thinking, right before Jesus invited them into his traveling salvation show, that they couldn't go on one more day—one more hour—in the soul-killing "small story" of their life. They needed to be dragged into a bigger story like they needed to breathe.

In my experience, the people who love Jesus the most are also the most desperate. That's borne out in Scripture, by the way. Look at a few of the people Jesus lavished praise on:

- The Roman centurion whose daughter was dying. ("I tell you the truth, I have not found anyone in Israel with such great faith"—Matthew 8:10.)
- The town prostitute who crashed a Pharisee's party so she could cover Jesus' feet with expensive perfume and her tears and then wipe them with her hair. ("Your faith has saved you; go in peace"—Luke 7:50.)
- The Canaanite woman who begged Jesus to cast a demon out of her daughter but first got only the cold shoulder from him and a comment about how he'd come for Israel's children, not dogs like her. ("Woman, you have great faith! Your request is granted"—Matthew 15:28.)
- The woman who was hemorrhaging blood, who sneaked up behind Jesus in a crowd and touched his cloak. ("Daughter, take courage; your faith has made you well"—Matthew 9:22, NASB.)

I think Oswald Chambers, in his classic devotional *My Utmost for His Highest*, has pinpointed why Jesus was so drawn to desperate people—he not only picked them out as his "volunteer team," he gravitated to them when he wanted to relax and enjoy himself. Here's part of what Chambers wrote for his June 25th entry, titled "Receiving Yourself in the Fires of Sorrow":

> Sorrow removes a great deal of a person's shallowness, but it does not always make that person better. Suffering either gives me to myself or it destroys me.
>
> You cannot find or receive yourself through success, because you lose your head over pride. And you cannot receive yourself through the monotony of your daily life, because you give in to complaining. The only way to find yourself is in the fires of sorrow. Why it should be this way is immaterial. The fact is that it is true in the Scriptures and in human experience. You can always recognize who has been through the fires of sorrow and received himself, and you know that you can go to him in your moment of trouble and find that he has plenty of time for you. But if a person has not been through the fires of sorrow, he is apt to be contemptuous, having no respect or time for you, only turning you away.
>
> If you will receive yourself in the fires of sorrow, God will make you nourishment for other people.[1]

The reason we look for Jesus-loving, desperate people to serve as volunteers in youth ministry is that they can offer "nourishment for other people." It's that simple. And oh, how today's teenagers need people who have "plenty of time" for them, who they can "go to in their moment of trouble." But how do you pick out the desperate Jesus lovers? Well, I think you've got to be one to know one. And when you are one, it's not hard to spot one.

Marinate in these comments from adult volunteers serving at exemplary youth ministries around the United States:

- *"If you are going to teach youth, they know if you love Jesus or not." (Travis Avenue Baptist Church, Fort Worth, Texas)*
- *"What our youth ministry has is a group of adults who are passionate about our relationship with Christ and we enjoy being with youth." (New Colony Baptist Church, Billerica, Massachusetts) A student at the same church said this about the adult leaders: "They're focused on God and that makes us want to be closer to God...It rubs off on us. They are a great example for us. We look up to them."*
- *"There's a passion [for Christ] that drives the leadership, each person involved has a passion...Those who have drifted haven't had the passion. It's not up to me to judge passion, but those who have stayed have an outspoken noticeable passion, and the kids pick up on that." (Rochester Covenant Church, Rochester, Minnesota)*

---

1 From *My Utmost for His Highest* by Oswald Chambers (Uhrichsville, OH: Barbour Publishing, 2006).

When I told my friend Bob Krulish that I was writing this book, he excitedly (and sheepishly) offered to give me something he thought would mesh perfectly with my Jesus-centered passions. When Bob talks, I always listen because he gushes truth. So I couldn't wait to get what he had for me.

What he slid across the table to me over coffee at a Panera Bread cafe was a real treasure—a condensed version of all the lessons he's learned in leading volunteers and ministry partners through more than 30 years as a top leader in Young Life and now as the director of pastoral ministry (a pastor to the pastoral staff) at my church. The document he gave me is titled "How Do We Think About Ministry?" and is subtitled "Nine Questions That Reveal Our Heart Motivation." (Bob tells me that he originally learned the leadership principles on this list from Doug Burleigh, former president of Young Life.)

I think Bob's one-page guide to leading leaders is the best thing I've ever seen on equipping volunteers in youth ministry—and it provides a specific road map for leading your desperate Jesus lovers in a Jesus-centered way.

Here's Bob's list, with my embellishments, applications, and illustrations:

1. What does my schedule say about how I think about ministry?

Do my leaders receive casual/crisis time or committed/caring thoughtful time?

My longtime friend Mark DeVries—a veteran youth minister, founder of Youth Ministry Architects, and a columnist for Group Magazine (and author of the Introduction to Chapter 13)—offers this insight into "casual time":

"The word 'delegate' literally means 'to send from one place to another.' Unfortunately, most youth pastors 'delegate' tasks and then essentially abandon volunteers to sink or swim on their own. Leaders who develop leaders walk alongside their volunteers and regularly check in with support and clarity, knowing how easily discouragement, misdirection, and fuzzy vision can prevent volunteers from completing the tasks they were originally asked to do."[2]

2. What do we do when we're together?

Does sarcasm, joking around, and cutting up characterize our times or does encouragement, exhortation, teaching, sharing, and training?

I love this sage advice from Jeanne Mayo, another three-decade youth pastor, Group columnist, and founder of Youth Source:

Gossip isn't our only dangerous enemy—its ugly cousin is sarcasm. Today's youth culture so loves humor that sarcasm is often viewed as a youth ministry friend rather than a foe, yet it's a "humor at any price" philosophy. Sarcasm mixes a measure of truth, then wraps it

---

2 From Mark DeVries' "Youth Ministry Consultant" column in the September/October 2006 issue of Group Magazine.

in barbed humor at someone else's expense. I've known many "cool" youth leaders who are quite adept at using sarcasm to communicate with teenagers. Proverbs 26:18-19 describes this behavior well: "Like a madman shooting firebrands or deadly arrows is a man who deceives his neighbor and says, 'I was only joking!' "

As I train youth leaders around the nation, I repeatedly tell them: "Please have the guts to drop the sarcasm when you joke around with your students. Train yourselves, as awkward as it might feel at first, to become a person who affirms others with your words. Though none of your teenagers will ever say it to you, they want your approval so much that they inwardly remember almost everything you say about them. You may know you're joking, but they don't."[3]

3. Does "expedience" or "maximizing" most characterize my leadership of people's lives?

Do I give frequent evaluation, encouragement, feedback, thanks, and affirmation? (*Your leaders' lips will answer that for us throughout the year of serving together—"Out of the abundance that fills the heart, the mouth speaks."*)

"We strive to have accountability together—we have accountability partners," says Rusty Comer, associate pastor for youth at New Colony Baptist Church (an exemplary youth ministry). "The [volunteer] staff meets once a month, and [we ask], 'Have you spent time with your students? How is your relationship with God?' "

4. What do our turnover statistics tell us?

Do people simply leave the ministry or are they called into another challenging ministry—with enthusiasm? Do they leave with bad or blasé feelings—feeling used, tired, frustrated—or do they value the experience and are better people for it?

Virtually every youth group in the exemplary youth ministry study has a team of long-term adult leaders as part of its "genius" mix of effective outreach to teenagers. When famed researcher Dr. Merton Strommen took a look at the results of the exemplary study, he found one engine for success was this: "Our effectiveness is due to the dedicated participation of volunteer adults and parents." And the key thing powering that engine was "their longevity—little turnover in personnel."[4]

One adult volunteer at First Presbyterian Church in Billings, Montana, simply says: "The genius here is the core experience of the leaders who have been here eight, 10 years or more."

5. Are we "people over program" or "program over people"?

Are those under my leadership growing and maximized in Christ? Do they

---

3 From Jeanne Mayo's article "The Ministry Killer," in the November/December 2004 issue of Group Magazine.

4 From "Exemplary Youth Ministry in Congregations Content Analysis Report: Pastor and Youth Minister," by Dr. Merton Strommen.

experience more of Christ because of their involvement? Or are they feeling pressured, frenetic, stressed, chaotic, and tense because of "ministry"? Does "tyranny of the urgent" characterize my leadership with people?

The fruit of this principle isn't hard to pluck—teenagers are great at noticing passion and growth in their adult leaders. One student at New Colony Baptist Church told an interviewer: "It's everyone's love for God around here...Seeing the youth leaders and how they live their lives with God is inspiring to us to live like they live."

Christian Smith, lead researcher for the *National Study of Youth and Religion*, says this: "The youth leaders who stood out in the minds of the teenagers we interviewed were not only those who took them to amusement parks and mission trips, but those who chatted on the phone with them in the evening, who were available to just hang out, and who knew and cared about their everyday crises."

6. How do I respond to correction or disagreement to those under my leadership?

Do I encourage it or kick against it? (*That is likely the way they will respond to me.*) Do I regularly ask for feedback from those I work with?

You wouldn't believe the development process for our youth ministry training events. After months of creative "baking," I roll out the first prototype of the workshop for a handful of youth ministry specialists and leaders at Group. I secretly call that first prototype rollout my "wood-chipper" day. After the five-hour presentation, we all get together and chop it up for a couple of hours. It's brutal, in the best sense of that word. More like "brutal for good"—that means there's plenty of precious blood on the floor. Then we do it all over again for youth pastors, again and again until it's what we want. In years past I've created up to 10 versions before we're all satisfied.

Over the years I've learned that these rip fests are brimming with great treasures I'd never get to hear if I were a pansy about it. Well, *I have* been a pansy about it sometimes. But now I've developed a strange aversion to wimpy criticism—"Come on, give me your best shot." I've also gotten much better about shunting away unhelpful or inaccurate criticism. The more criticism-friendly the environment, the more likely you are to find the very input that moves your thing from good to great.

7. How easy is it for a prospective leader to climb aboard?

How easy is it for them to leave? What is the correlation between the two in our thinking?

Mark DeVries consults with churches in need of youth ministry help all the time. He says: "Make sure that leadership development is at the top of your daily to-do list. As I coach our youth ministry clients, I almost always ask them for recruiting updates. Here's a typical response: 'Have I told you about how great the weather is around here?' Let's face it. Recruiting and developing leaders is the hardest part of most youth workers' jobs. And therefore, the average youth worker puts off recruitment until other tasks have been accomplished. If you wait to recruit volunteers until the need is urgent, you're guaranteed to be in a chronic volunteer crisis."

8. How do I think about growth?

Do I approach it from primarily an organizational standpoint (mass recruiting, high profile, goal setting, number orientation) or an organism perspective (prayer—Matthew 9:36-38; taking care of and nurturing the people we have—Luke 19:12-27; the body building the body—Ephesians 4:16)? Fulfilled, enthusiastic people will recruit others into the ministry.

I think this comment from a teenager at New Colony Baptist Church is telling: "There are a ton of people in the church that have a strong passion for God...I love everyone in this church, and one thing that's helped me through my walk with Jesus is whenever I'm slipping away someone here notices and they take time out of their lives to talk to me, make me feel better, get me back on the right track."

9. Take care of your leaders.

At the end of the year they ought to be able to say: "Wow, what a great year. I know the Lord more intimately than ever before. My faith is greater. I've grown and been trained in serving him."

John Wooden, hall-of-fame coach of the great UCLA basketball teams in the 1960s, made his players *both* better people and better basketball players. That word got out to every basketball player in America. Because he "took care of his leaders," he didn't even have to recruit. Everyone wanted to come and be with him. This ought to be our Christ-like standard of ministry. If we can't offer this, then we're just "using" people. And God doesn't "use" people, even though one of our favorite prayers in the church is for God to "use" us. You'll never find God "using" people in Scripture, but you will find him partnering with them, moving through them, fighting alongside them, and commissioning them. Those are great (and true) words to express our Jesus-centered passions with volunteer leaders, too.

Parents

(WITH AN INTRODUCTION BY MARK DEVRIES)

WHERE WOULD MY KIDS BE WITHOUT YOUTH MINISTRY?

If you measured youth ministry years like dog years (seven youth ministry years for every normal human year), I'm a geezer—217 years old, to be exact.

I taught my first parenting seminar at the wise old age of 20. Like a spring-loaded trap, I was happy to give this group of unsuspecting parents a piece of my mind, to let them know the ways they were massively missing the mark with their children.

Today, I see things differently.

I'm a recovering parent of teenagers—two are growing into their adult lives and one is slated to sprint through high school graduation in just a few months. Today I see how parents have become the easy whipping boy of youth ministry. Too many youth workers (and youth ministry experts) rail against the failures of parents—failure to make their kids come to church, failure to keep their mouths shut when they feel like complaining, and failure to "support the youth ministry" (which often means an unwillingness to go on a weekend retreat when we ask them at the last minute).

As a youth worker who's also a parent, I've got no doubt which is the harder (and more important) job. When I do parenting seminars, I see desperation on so many faces—enough to know that parents of teenagers are an exhausted lot. Like test animals enduring inconsistent shock therapy, these parents are jumpy, anxious, nervous about the new, latest threat to their children's safety (and thus to their own parental sanity).

The sad fact is that the blame game (youth workers blaming parents and parents blaming youth workers) helps neither families nor youth ministries. We need each other.

As a youth worker, it didn't take me long to realize that I could never build a thriving ministry without partnering with parents. As a parent, it didn't take me long to realize that relying on my own inconsistent parenting skills was not the recipe for producing the kind of faith maturity I prayed to see in my own children. I shudder to think where my kids would be today apart from their church.

Adam was always a good kid—creative, funny, and always the guy who knew how to be a friend. But it was his friendship with his youth leader Julian that fired his faith and led him down a path to claiming an intimate relationship with Christ (and a ministry calling) for himself.

Debbie, our busy dancer, didn't always have time to be at every youth group meeting. But Elaine and Jen were adults who, by their contagious examples, kept (and still keep) Debbie on a path where following Christ is as natural as the air she breathes.

Our soon-to-be-adult Leigh continues to be profoundly impacted by the godly friendship of Erika—10 years her senior but always her first choice for advice. Taylor, Piper, Ellie, and a dozen or so other Christian adults helped keep Leigh in the game on those days when she considered trading in her own family for a newer model.

I shudder to think where my children would be without their church. As a parent, I needed the youth ministry as much as, and maybe more than, my kids did.

This is a world that literally dis-integrates teenagers, forcing them into premature patchwork identities that grow out of disconnected relationships with adults who know nothing of each other (coaches who don't know the pastors who don't know the parents who don't know the teachers who don't know...). The centrifugal force pulling kids away from a convergent center in which they can develop an integrated identity is so powerful that it is perhaps only in a faith community that young people in today's world can complete the identity formation process.

Our children's identity was formed not out of our parenting ingenuity but as part and parcel of a life surrounded by a convergent community of adults who knew and respected each other. These adults affirmed similar standards, values, and expectations—they modeled a consistent message around which my children's lives could be ordered. From this side of the parenting journey, I realize now that my primary job as a youth worker is not to be a camp counselor, not simply to build one-on-one relationships with each young person. I realize my primary work is to be an architect, helping to build a constellation of relationships with Christ-like adults for every teenager in my program.

One parent told me the experience of parenting teenagers feels like "being a dachshund in deep snow." I can relate. I've learned enough now to know that God never meant for us to do this parenting thing alone, especially parenting teenagers.

I shudder to think where my kids would be without their youth ministry.

—MARK DeVries
Youth Ministry Architects, and Associate Pastor for Youth and Their Families,
First Presbyterian Church, Nashville, Tennessee

f there's an undeniable truth in youth ministry today, it's that God has ordained parents to be the key catalysts in a teenager's first and ongoing commitment to Christ. Parents are, by far, the biggest influence on their teenagers' faith. I recently asked the *National Study of Youth and Religion's* Dr. Christian Smith to pluck something from the study that would affect the way youth pastors see parents in their ministry. Here's what he wrote:

> Teens' parents and other mature Christian adults need to be brought back into the youth ministry picture. In most cases, parents are the most important Christian pastors teenagers will ever have—for better or worse. Yet for decades, youth ministry's conventional wisdom has separated young people from adults. My observations suggest that there's an important and legitimate place for age-exclusive church youth groups. Yet many parents also come to see designated youth ministers as substitutes for their own 'pastoral' responsibilities. They check in their teenagers at youth group and assume all is well.
>
> Many youth ministers are frustrated by this "service provider" mentality in parents, and that makes them antagonistic toward them. But this adversarial situation must be replaced by a more cooperative, integrated, comprehensive approach to the faith formation of young people.

In short, if you want to impact your teenagers deeply for Christ, to draw kids more deeply into a Jesus-centered lifestyle, few things are more important than impacting their parents. Researchers, youth ministry leaders, and culture watchers are now all shouting with one voice—ministry to and with parents is the key to kids' long-term devotion to Jesus. But clarity doesn't always translate to priority. Some years ago I asked youth pastors all over the world to tell me their top complaints about their work—here's what they said:

1. "Lack of parental involvement"...54 percent
2. "Bad attitudes"...10 percent
3. (tie) "Your pastor" and "Too busy"...9 percent
4. (tie) "Volunteers" and "Salary"...6 percent
5. "Other church staffers"...4 percent
6. "The church bus"...3 percent[1]

Wow, that's a landslide election. If I were a parent of a teenager, I'd be feeling the heat at church. And that's just the problem—there's heat on both sides, and that often gets in the way of what we *both* have to do to draw kids into more intimate

---

1 From a Group Magazine survey of American youth pastors in 2000, published in my "Youth Ministry Minute" column in the November/December 2000 issue.

relationships with Jesus. Jesus-centered youth ministry is not easy to do when parents often seem like your enemies, not your teammates. It'd be nice if we had a magic potion we could slip into their Venti Starbucks to make them friends instead of enemies, but Jesus had a better way:

"You have heard that it was said, 'Love your neighbor and hate your enemy.' But I tell you: Love your enemies and pray for those who persecute you, that you may be sons of your Father in heaven" (Matthew 5:43-45a).

LOVING OUR SO-CALLED ENEMIES

When parents are acting less like our neighbors and more like our enemies, that's a glorious opportunity to behave like Jesus and give evidence that we're sons and daughters of a God who "causes the rain to fall on the just and the unjust." Loving the parents of the teenagers in our groups will mean we're doggedly determined to connect with them, equip them to deepen their kids' pursuit of Jesus, and serve them.

1. Connect with them.

I've often said that a mediocre parent—someone who's at least *trying* to disciple his or her teenager—can out-impact the best youth leader on the planet. That's because a parent's influence can dwarf any other. So if you can move a parent off the sidelines of discipling and into the game by simply connecting with him or her more often, you've just made a permanent impact on a teenager.

Mike Gibson, a youth and children's minister in Richland Hills, Texas, says: "We try to consistently pursue relationships with the parents. There is no program—just an ongoing attempt to make contact with parents to see how things are going in their families, at work, and so on. We talk to some parents when they pick up their students, and contact others by phone. When we're consistent, we can tell a difference in their attitude toward the ministry."

Kandi Fernandez, a youth leader in Tampa, Florida, says: "We have quarterly parents meetings to explain what will be happening in the next three months. We also hand out printed calendars of events, fund-raisers, retreats, and other activities we've planned. We ask at each meeting that parents provide their names, addresses, phone numbers, and e-mail addresses so our records are current. And we send out e-mail reminders to the parents about upcoming events."

And Fort Gibson, Oklahoma, youth leader Todd Vick says: "I keep my parents involved in the youth ministry through an online discussion board. It's a way to keep them connected and up-to-date on information. Not only can parents log on and see what's going on in the ministry, but they can also connect with each other and get parenting advice."

2. Equip them to deepen their kids' pursuit of Jesus.

The first book I ever wrote was in partnership with a genius youth minister named Ben Freudenburg. I helped Ben translate his vision and practice for equipping parents as the primary faith catalysts in their kids' lives into the book *The Family Friendly Church*. Ben's experience in moving his church from a traditional youth ministry structure to a parent-equipping structure was long and fraught with difficulties, like any pioneering effort would be. But Ben's vision is transforming because it's so rooted in a Jesus-centered truth—Christ said "honor your father and mother," and Ben says, "The home is the primary agency for faith formation."[2]

Among many other innovations, Ben and his staff came up with a strategy for planting his "home-centered, church-supported" vision in the church. The idea was to scrutinize some of the faith-deepening practices of a traditional youth ministry and brainstorm how some of those ideas could be morphed into something parents do instead, with a lot of equipping help from the church.

The best example of this idea I've ever seen is actually happening at my own church in Denver—it's called The Wild Challenge and was created by my friend Doug Ashley, the church's middle school family pastor. Essentially, The Wild Challenge is an experiential adventure for fathers of 13-year-old sons. For the first month, the fathers meet with each other to read and discuss *Wild at Heart*, by John Eldredge. Then, for the next five months, fathers engage their sons about five key biblical issues—for example, "What Is Success?"

Once a month, fathers take their sons on an experience that will help them dig into that month's issue. For the issue of "Success," they go car shopping at a number of dealerships. Doug gives them an overview of what to do, along with suggested discussion questions. Then, during the day, the fathers engage in a natural discussion about success, including the Bible's view of it. Later that month, all the fathers and sons get together for a field trip. The Success field trip was to a football stadium where a Christian NFL player talked about true success, followed by a lunchtime discussion fueled by questions at each table.

At the end of six months, fathers and sons gather for a blessing banquet—fathers choose a symbol to give to their sons that represents how they see them, and then they tell their sons why they're proud of who they are. That's right, it's a real tear-jerker. Doug's subversive intent is to give fathers lots of practice talking to their sons about faith issues and their everyday relationship with Jesus. There's also a similar mother-daughter adventure at the church, geared for activities that women and young girls relate to. (By the way, Doug translated his vision into a practical handbook for pulling off the program—it's called, simply, *The Wild Challenge*[3] and is available from Group Publishing.)

The hidden engine driving the success of Doug's Wild Challenge idea is something I call "Practicing Congruence." I first heard "congruence" described as a crucial life practice over breakfast one morning with Tom Melton.

---

2 From *The Family Friendly Church* by Ben Freudenburg and Rick Lawrence (Loveland, CO: Group Publishing, 1998).

3 Doug Ashley, *The Wild Challenge* (Loveland, CO: Group Publishing, 2004).

"Congruence," he said, "is when you're the same person—with the same priorities, passions, and personality—in every arena in your life. When you're not spending energy adapting yourself to every competing arena, you have a lot more energy to make an impact in those arenas. It means living on the outside what is true on the inside."

Essentially, a congruent life means *what you say* is *who you are*, and it's evident from your choices and functional priorities. So a few weeks ago I decided to give all the teenagers in my church a secret "Congruence Survey" that targeted their parents— I gave them three questions to answer that focused on what their parents *say* is most important in life, what their *actions* communicate is most important in life, and what their family's functional "motto" is. When I collected all the surveys, I found only six kids—four junior highers and two senior highers—could say that their parents are congruent about a "hub" relationship with Jesus—I mean, only six said their parents *say* their faith in Christ is most important and back it up with their *example*. There was evidence of congruence around other beliefs and practices—school excellence, trying hard in life, and honoring family, for example—but living a congruent life around the hub of Jesus is a rare experience in most families.

So, when Doug created a way for fathers to not only *talk* about their faith in Christ with their sons, but *show* their sons how important Jesus is to their everyday life, he was helping them move toward congruence. And a congruent parent wields an unstoppable influence. When you're congruent, you create something like a gravitational center that exerts unseen "pull" on the people within that gravitational field. And when your family is congruent around a passion for Christ, the kids tend to orbit around Christ the rest of their lives.

Now the overarching point here is to take inventory of what you're already doing in youth ministry—retreats, mission trips, Bible studies, small groups, service projects, camps—and brainstorm ways you might possibly equip parents to partner in (or even take over) each activity. In every case, your goal is to move them toward greater congruence in the way they relate with their teenagers. Some quick one-off examples:

- *Retreats*—Use a team of parent speakers (a large number such as six) as your surprise "big name" retreat speaker. Ask them to each offer a story-filled presentation on what "determined to know nothing but Christ and him crucified" looks like in their everyday life.
- *Mission Trips*—Every year plan one mission trip that's just for families—use evenings on the trip to get families laughing and learning together.
- *Bible Studies*—Hold your "going deeper" Bible study in a different parent's home every week, and ask the host parent(s) to participate on "their night."
- *Small Groups*—Once a month (or once every two months) ask for at least one parent of every teenager in your small groups to come to a meeting with their teenager to experience it together.

- *Service Projects*—Ben Freudenburg used to plan one service project a year that was tailored for whole families—they planned and presented the church's VBS from the previous summer to native Alaskan Indians. Ben says, "We plunged families into situations that demanded conflict resolution, forgiveness, and teamwork. And we helped them create a memory they'll never forget."

  Yvonne Zielaznicki, a youth leader in Bridgewater, New Jersey, says: "We collect health and school supplies all year for Church World Services' Have a Heart program—we put together supply kits to give away to needy families. Then we invite our families for an 'assembly day' to pack the kits (we serve them lunch). The adults oversee the piles of supplies while the kids go around the room collecting what they need for each kit."
- *Camps*—Lots of camps are now offering family camp options as part of their summer menu. Find one near you and be the point person for recruiting families to go—you'll help even more if you plan a creative fund-raiser to help defray costs of the camp.

3. Serve them.

Cindy Golding, a youth minister in Cedar Rapids, Iowa, says: "We offer a popular parenting class to the parents of our teenagers. It started out as a request from one of the youth's mothers. She said she felt 'out of her league' when it came to parenting her 13-year-old daughter. She asked for my help as a mentor (I'm the mother of six kids, and her daughter and mine are great friends). My friend said she wanted to have the same confidence in dealing with her daughter that she saw when I interacted with the youth group kids. I had to share my little secret—my confidence came from watching and learning from older, more experienced parents when my children were young. Our parenting class is more than just lessons—it's a mentoring group. The parents learn about what's 'normal' and gain the confidence they need to do their tough parenting job."

You can also serve parents by simply encouraging them. Jane Gamroth, a youth leader in Edmonton, Alberta, says: "To connect with parents, our youth leadership team hangs around after the service to talk with them about their kids. We find positive, uplifting things to tell them. For example, we talk about how their children are helping others, or how they've stepped up and represented Christ today, or the improvement we've seen in their ability to pay attention during youth group. I've occasionally called and left messages for parents on their home phone, thanking them for their children's contribution that particular Sunday."

If you keep yourself busy "loving your enemies," you'll have little time to think about your complaints, and you might just get to witness one of the great moments in ministry—a parent making a deep impact on their teenager's passion for Jesus.

Jesus-centered ministry both honors and energizes the powerful, dominating role parents play in their kids' maturation into Christ followers—and it also honors the role of "true family" in kids' lives. Here's what I mean.

The desperate people Jesus hung around with became his family—people he would refer to as his *true* mother, brother, and sisters. It's right there in Scripture:

> *While Jesus was still talking to the crowd, his mother and brothers stood outside, wanting to speak to him. Someone told him, "Your mother and brothers are standing outside, wanting to speak to you." He replied to him, "Who is my mother, and who are my brothers?" Pointing to his disciples, he said, "Here are my mother and my brothers. For whoever does the will of my Father in heaven is my brother and sister and mother"* (Matthew 12:46-50).

A little earlier in Matthew, Jesus made this startling proclamation:

> *Do not suppose that I have come to bring peace to the earth. I did not come to bring peace, but a sword. For I have come to turn "a man against his father, a daughter against her mother, a daughter-in-law against her mother-in-law—a man's enemies will be the members of his own household." Anyone who loves his father or mother more than me is not worthy of me; anyone who loves his son or daughter more than me is not worthy of me.* (Matthew 10:34-38).

Then again, later in Matthew, Jesus reiterated what's true about our family, and what's not: "And do not call anyone on earth 'father,' for you have one Father, and he is in heaven" (Matthew 23:9).

Sin tore us away from our true Father—that's why Jesus told the Pharisees they were of "your father, the devil" (John 8:44). But our true Father found a way to adopt us back into his very own family. This is why Jesus publicly refers to God as "your Father" and to his followers as "brothers and sisters and daughters and sons."

Now, as I mentioned earlier, this is also the same Jesus who told his disciples (twice in Matthew—chapters 15 and 19) to "honor your father and mother." So what gives?

Well, it's not an either/or situation. It's a both/and situation. Jesus-centered ministry helps build deep connections among the members of our teenagers' true family—the brothers, sisters, mothers, and fathers they've been "grafted into" as fellow Christ followers—and it helps "build up in Christ" their DNA family by proactively connecting with their parents.

Let me close this chapter by reemphasizing something Christian Smith said at the beginning:

> *"In most cases, parents are the most important Christian pastors teenagers will ever have—for better or worse."*

This is good news, because God has handed you an opportunity to partner with parents, whenever possible, to lay the groundwork for a Christ-following life for their kids. The more ways you find to partner with your teenagers' parents and other caring adults in your church family, the more likely you are to connect kids with life-transforming impact. So don't let preconceived notions or past failures stop you from making that connection between parents and your youth ministry—and start building up the True Family in the DNA Families of your kids today.

Communication

COMMUNICATING IN R.E.A.L. WAYS

We often hear a certain term assigned to a person considered a famed, top-of-the-game youth pastor. He or she is called a "great communicator."

What do people mean when they use that term? Generally, they mean the admired youth pastor delivers polished lectures, keeps an audience's attention for a period of time, and often hears "I really enjoyed your talk."

In short, a "great communicator" is an entertainer. He or she provides a pleasant or interesting presentation for a passive audience. Entertainment is a nice thing. Great communicators are nice to have around. A good lecture is more pleasant than a boring one. But is entertainment the goal of a Jesus-centered youth ministry? Was the impact and lasting effectiveness of Jesus' ministry hinged on a reputation akin to today's definition of a "great communicator"?

We think not. In fact, we're concerned much of the youth ministry world has been sold a lie, with all good intentions. Many youth workers look longingly at the higher profile of their senior pastors and somehow conclude that ministry success looks like a riveting speaker enthralling an adoring but passive audience.

But that's not Jesus-centered ministry. That's a ministry model borrowed from the entertainment world—and the academic world. In the centuries following Jesus' ministry, the keepers of the church began to view faith as a subject to be mastered, much like any other subject such as literature or history. So, the thinking went, if we have a subject to teach, we need a studious professor and rows of passive students to hear the fact-filled lectures.

The trouble is, faith in our Lord Jesus Christ is not a subject to be mastered. Faith is a relationship. Not an academic subject. Or a show. The nurture of a relationship looks a lot more like a friendship than it does a history class or a stage presentation. The goal of a great relationship is not the accumulation of factual knowledge or the applause of an entertained crowd. The goal of a great relationship is an ever-deepening love, trust, and commitment to one another that demonstrates itself through self-sacrifice.

Jesus didn't come to Earth to be a "great communicator." He came to nurture life's most important relationship. He did that through many different ways. He sometimes communicated truths in front of a crowd. He also mentored one-to-one, led a small group, told stories, used visual aids, challenged his friends with tough questions, and led his people through highly memorable experiences in order to cement the relationship.

So, what can we learn about communicating in a Jesus-centered youth ministry? That communication, if it is to be truly effective and life-changing, must be R.E.A.L. That is, it must be Relational, Experiential, Applicable, and Learner-based:

- *Relational.* Communication (and relationship) is greatly enhanced when everyone gets to talk. In a youth ministry setting, you may set up a message with a story and then ask students to unwrap it with one another in pairs or small groups, giving everyone a time to talk.
- *Experiential.* People learn—and change—by doing. Jesus knew this. That's why he used so many memorable experiences: washing the disciples' feet, calming a storm, mixing spit in the dirt to make a healing mud, and so on. In youth ministry, we can employ simple (or exotic) experiences to captivate, teach, and inspire our students. Just as Jesus did.
- *Applicable.* Effective communication in a Jesus-centered youth ministry is not about information. It's about transformation. So, our communication needs to center around life application. No student should leave our communication without a clear idea of how to implement today's message into everyday life.
- *Learner-based.* It's not about you. It's about your kids—and their relationship with Jesus. It doesn't matter how you were taught, how you like to learn, or how you're comfortable teaching. It's not about you. Just as Jesus did, we need to adapt our approach to how our students will most effectively be reached.

Effective communication in ministry—and in a great relationship—has little to do with becoming a silver-tongued entertainer or a know-it-all professor. Effective communication in ministry looks a lot like the kinds of communicating found in a healthy friendship.

—THOM SCHULTZ
Founder and CEO of Group Publishing
—JOANI SCHULTZ
Chief Creative Officer of Group Publishing

As Thom and Joani Schultz said in their introduction to this chapter, you'd be hard-pressed to find a youth minister who doesn't use some kind of lecture strategy as the focal point for communicating the gospel to kids. The youth sermon is the quintessential cross-denominational ministry practice, and has been since Rick Warren was purpose-less. But in my many years as editor of Group Magazine, I never published an article on youth talk ideas or strategies until just a few years ago—and that piece was my attempt to offer more effective alternative ways to "lecture."

There's a mountain of research that discounts lecturing as an effective way to help people learn, especially young people (you'll find all the backup you need on this truth in the Schultzes' two groundbreaking books *Why Nobody Learns Much of Anything at Church* and *The Dirt on Learning*). But that's not all. Even if you're a big believer in youth talks, you be hard-pressed to point to many sermons or messages that actually changed your life. Life change is almost always the result of an experience followed by some kind of debriefing.

I could use my fingernail to drive a screw into a piece of wood (ouch, I've tried it), but I'd rather use something that's more effective...like, say, a screwdriver. In theory, almost all youth leaders agree. When I asked youth ministers around the world to tell me how they teach their kids spiritual truths, "youth talks or messages" ranked dead last in a list of six strategies—only 5 percent made sermons their top choice.[1] Even so, I know from our own ongoing research that seven out of 10 youth leaders include the fingernail-like youth talk in a typical youth group meeting[2] (and the other three are telling a white lie, I think).

Though youth talks are incredibly popular, they're not all that effective. So why are so many using them? Well, I asked youth leaders in our youthministry .com online community to tell me why the youth-talk practice, like a post-bomb cockroach, has survived for so long. They said:

1. Sermons require less time, work, creativity, and risk.
2. Youth talks are traditional in ministry—"that's how we were trained to teach, and we've always done it that way."
3. There are (supposedly) few resources that help youth leaders teach in active and interactive ways.
4. It's all an issue of control—youth talks keep the control in the youth leader's hands.

Now that I've hauled into the light the reasons why youth leaders continue to use a proven ineffective practice to communicate with teenagers, it's time to point our noses back toward Jesus.

In our youth ministry training events, I ask youth pastors to find a partner in the crowd and share about "something you've learned that has deeply impacted your life—something that turned your life around." They each get a couple of minutes to do it, and then I ask everyone to close their eyes. Next, I ask them to

---

1 From a Group Magazine survey of American youth pastors in 2000, published in an article I wrote titled "What's the Deal With Youth Talks," in the November/December 2000 issue.

2 From a Group Magazine demographic survey of subscribers in 2004.

raise their hands if they *primarily* communicated their profound learning using principles, or if they did it by *primarily* telling a story.

I've done this many times now, and I always find a 25/75 split in the crowd—25 percent taught using principles and 75 percent taught using stories. In my experience, the percentages are exactly flipped in the church—three-quarters of us primarily teach using principles; only a quarter (at best) primarily teach using stories. So, when we don't realize we're "teaching," why do three-quarters of us naturally use stories instead of principles?

Because our hearts understand something our heads refuse to accept.

Experiences give us our deepest, longest-lasting lessons in life. That's why we're so fascinated by stories, and why Jesus used stories (parables) and experiences to teach so often. In fact, his principle-to-story ratio was probably more like 20/80. People are riveted by stories, but they have to work to pay attention to principles. The Beatitudes in Matthew 5 were based on *principles of truth*; the parables throughout the gospels were *stories of truth*.

We experience the power behind story-based communicating every week—the next time you're listening to your pastor give a sermon, pay attention to the difference in the congregation when the pastor is teaching "principles" and when the pastor tells a real-life story. It's often rather noisy during principle time, but incredibly quiet during story time.

Here's what I'm getting at: *We way overuse principle-based teaching and way under-use story-based teaching and experiences.*

THE POWER OF PARABLES

Every parable Jesus told was crafted to answer one or both of two questions: "Who is God?" and "What is life in his kingdom like?" In fact, in many cases, Jesus started his parables with "The kingdom of God is like..." Jesus-centered communicating influences us to shift from teaching that expounds on principles to teaching that uses stories—or experiences—that point to God's character and way of life. That means we become voracious hoarders of stories and experiences that communicate Jesus' true personality and character.

Teaching using experiences simply means we use real-life experiences as a launching pad for teaching (World Vision's 24-Hour Famine, for example, paves the way for teaching about the purpose of fasting and Jesus' emphasis on caring for the poor), or we create contrived experiences as a launching pad for teaching (for example, the American slang game from earlier in this book).

Teaching using parables simply means we use our own stories, and the stories of others, to reveal who God is, and what life is like in his kingdom.

Here's how this works, baby step by baby step.

First, you think of one story in your life that's captured your attention—you still remember it because it was memorable. For example, just the other day I was driving down the highway during rush hour and saw a bunch of papers swirling around—getting chewed up in the traffic. I passed an offramp, where I saw a guy getting out of his car to grab the last few sheets of paper stuck on the back of his car—he'd obviously stacked his important papers on his car when he left home, then forgot they were there. I remember that story because I put myself in his shoes—it was a heartbreaking scene.

After a story pops into your head, you write a brief description of it. Then you ask God to show you the "parable connection" to this story. I don't mean that you connect it to one of Jesus' parables. I mean, how could this story teach others something about who God is, or what life in his kingdom is like?

For example, in my story the parable connection I came up with has to do with the consequences of my sin—I can be forgiven, but like that paper scattered all over the highway, I can't keep the effects of my sin from spreading—I can't get that consequence back.

This practice of "mining parables" from your life can be part of your everyday life with God. One popular retreat speaker has been doing this for years—she keeps a condensed list of her life parables with her and asks God to show her which stories to tell before every speaking engagement, and she's constantly adding to the list.

As you move through your daily experiences, ask God to show you your parables. God didn't stop telling parables when the canon of the Bible was closed—he's still telling his story by every means possible. And we can branch out from our own stories to "mine parables" from the lives of our friends, family, ministry partners, and teenagers in our ministry.

The practical way to make sure this happens is to keep a "story journal"—something you keep with you to collect memorable stories that, by God's grace, you connect to a parable truth. Five minutes before the end of your workday, simply write one-sentence descriptions of the stories and experiences you've encountered that day. After that, or at the end of the week, ask God to show you the parables locked up in your stories. For each one God shows you, write a bit of a longer description in your story journal—this will help you build up a "treasure chest" of parables to use in your teaching, your conversations, your counseling sessions—really, everything you do.

STEALING FROM THE PARABLE VAULT

There's a rich vault full of parables that I haven't even mentioned—I've referenced it many times already in this book. That vault is full of...films.

There are literally millions of parables buried in the films and videos our kids are ingesting right now. Not everything in these films is a parable, of course—but God has shrewdly buried clues about himself in the most unexpected places. It's up to us to find them and use them to point kids back to who Jesus really is, and what living in his kingdom is really like.

Jesus constantly mined parables from the culture of his day—remember the parable of the Laborers in the Field, the Weeds and the Wheat, and the Pearl of

Great Price? These stories were directly drawn from Jesus' cultural influences—they were very familiar to those he was trying to teach. If we're awake to the parables that surround us, we can use them as door openers to the deepest places in kids' hearts.

There are four ways to "mine" the culture for parables.

- First, teach your kids to understand what you're looking for, and have them bring you possible parables.
- Second, no matter what you're listening to or watching, be alert for parables and extract them to use in your ministry.
- Third, there are places we can find video parables that didn't exist a couple of years ago—including the Web sites www.YouTube.com and www.GoFish .com. These sites are like vaults for all kinds of videos—both professionally produced and homegrown. They are not Christian sites, so be aware of that. But you can use them to search for parable moments.
- Fourth, as I've mentioned earlier, we've created an entire Web site that gives you already-extracted parables from kids' cultural influences and then pairs them with some great discussion questions. It's called MinistryandMedia .com, and I think it's one of the very best youth ministry tools in the world.

KEEPING THE BABY, NOT THE BATH WATER

No matter what I say, message giving will still be central to the ministry DNA of many youth leaders—maybe you. So why not play with some ways to make them more infected with Christ-like impact? Try these ideas:

1. Inject small-group discussions into your message time.
Texas youth leader Andrew Carpenter says, "We do a small-group discussion after the talk, led by volunteers. This allows kids to process what they just heard, saw, learned, or experienced."

2. Engage kids with experiential learning activities before, during, or after the talk.
Virginia youth leader Joe Bradford says he sets up his youth talks with activities that surprise and entice kids into the truth. "I let them find the 'Aha!' in their own minds," says Bradford. "For example, I did a lesson on the body as God's temple. I first had them do a quiz—they won pretzels for right answers. After a while I said, 'Oh, I'm sorry, you must be thirsty.' We had been talking about tattoos, movies, and body piercing. When my helper came back, she had a gallon of water with a little dirt in the bottom. They all cried out, 'Eew!' And I replied, 'What's wrong? It just has a little dirt in it!' That had been their approach to R-rated movies, tattoos, and so on. They put two and two together, not me."

3. Use games, drama, or object lessons to spark discussion.
Many youth leaders use skits, themed games, and even visual illustrations

to kick off a discussion that flows into a youth talk. Chris Merwin says, "Team-building games are a great way to teach them that they need to rely on more than themselves to accomplish things." Oklahoma youth leader Sammye Rogers says, "We have found incorporating drama and object lessons with the message drives home the point and opens the hearts of the youth to receive the Word. Most of the dramas and object lessons are humorous, but to the point."

4. Use "group explorations" instead.

Alabama youth minister Joey Fine says, "I tell my youth that it's going to be a group discussion and that they are the lesson. I give them a topic about a spiritual issue to explore, and they sometimes discover more than I have!" Eliza Rutter adds, "I use a lot of group work where kids discover spiritual truths on their own. I like to ask questions or give kids an outrageous situation to get the group talking. We often brainstorm things by writing down our ideas, then we go back over our lists together. The youth can learn a great deal from each other without me ever saying a word."

The overarching truth about the way Jesus communicated is simple: He used methods that worked for those he was trying to reach, not methods that served his own needs. Paul says Jesus "emptied Himself, taking the form of a bond-servant" (Philippians 2:7, NASB) as he launched himself into his Father's grand rescue mission. And every time we "decrease ourselves" in favor of "increasing communication," we're soaking teenagers in the spirit of Jesus.

Part Three

CLOSING
IMPERATIVES

Determined to Know Nothing

Yesterday I went to a presentation by Dr. David Walsh, founder and president of the National Institute on Media and Family (www.mediawise.org). He's a much-interviewed and respected secular expert on the impact of media on children and teenagers. Walsh is not only a brilliant apostle for the scientific study of the media's powerful ability to teach, but he's also passionate in his opposition to the media's abuse of "storytelling" power in kids' lives. His motto: "Whoever tells the stories defines the culture."

Right now, says Walsh, the storytellers are defining our culture by teaching kids that these should be our primary values:

- More
- Fast
- Easy
- Fun[1]

> "If the Jesus we've embraced and taught is really a neutered Jesus, we've plunged kids into deeper confusion."

It's no wonder that so many teenagers (and adults) see Jesus through these filters. Many of us want Jesus to give us more of what we want, we want him to do it fast and make it easy for us, and we want guarantees that our fun won't be compromised if we follow him. If we allow ourselves and our teenagers to be fashioned by the false storytellers in our culture, we'll end up graduating class after class of young Pharisees—teenagers who are pragmatically associated with the benefits of "religion," but not desperately in love with Jesus.

One of the most haunting things Jesus ever said is in Matthew 6:22-23: "The eye is the lamp of the body. If your eyes are good, your whole body will be full of

---

1 From a presentation by Dr. David Walsh to the Cherry Creek School District's "Parent Information Network" meeting in Denver, Colorado on October 3, 2006.

light. But if your eyes are bad, your whole body will be full of darkness. If then the light within you is darkness, how great is that darkness!"

My translation of this for beeline youth ministry is, simply: If the Jesus we've embraced and taught is really a neutered Jesus, we've plunged kids into deeper confusion. It's the principle of the Trojan horse I discussed earlier in this book.

WHAT'S OUR STORY?

I couldn't agree more with Walsh's "storyteller" motto, and that's why it's so crucial to pay close attention to the "story" we're telling teenagers about Jesus. This is why Spurgeon's beeline is such a crucial guide and metaphor—if we "beeline" everything we do back to Jesus, we might have a shot at remembering him for who he is.

Put another way, if our primary pursuit, like the Apostle Paul's, is to "determine to know nothing but Christ, and him crucified," we'll naturally help kids develop a countercultural mind-set about their lives. How can you believe (for too long) that life is essentially about "more, fast, easy, and fun" when everything you do at church is somehow connected back to Christ crucified?

Not long ago I was talking with Ron Belsterling, an associate professor of Christian education and youth ministry at Nyack College in New York, about an experience he had as he was pursuing his doctoral degree—it had profoundly sealed his perspective on the power of Jesus-centered mentoring. As part of a doctoral project, Ron had convinced a church to experiment with an outreach trip that targeted a nearby inner-city neighborhood instead of the youth group's traditional overseas trip that included four days of "ministry" and six days of fun on the beach. Parents who were fine about their kids going on a cross-cultural mission/fun trip were very worried about them walking the streets of an urban neighborhood that was just 20 minutes away.

One night Ron and the kids on his inner-city outreach looked out the window of their hotel and saw two men viciously kicking a woman who was high on drugs, and therefore unable to defend herself or run away. Ron turned to these protected, wide-eyed middle-class kids and asked, "What are we going to do about this?"

The kids said, "Well, we can't go down there!"

Ron answered, "Why not? *Down there* is where Jesus would be."

The kids responded: "What can we do? The only thing we know how to do is sing!" (Most of the kids on the outreach were part of the church's respected youth choir.)

Ron fired back, "Well, let's go down there and sing then. We'll give what Jesus has given us to give."

So the whole group trooped down to the street, stood on the opposite sidewalk, and started singing. The two guys kicking the woman looked up, startled, and then immediately ran away in fear. The woman then crawled across the street and lay down in the middle of the kids as they continued singing.

That night, those kids followed the beeline that Ron found for them—they learned what it's like to be rescuers, just like Jesus. And the wall separating their faith from their real life crumbled a little more.

Saturation is the key to the beeline—the "storytellers" in our culture are raising the waterline of what's considered "normal" by saturating us with messages about "more, fast, easy, and fun." So what might happen if *we raised the waterline* in our ministries by saturating our teenagers with the beeline to Christ in even the most mundane, obscure things we do. For example:

- *Language*—What if we changed the way we talk with teenagers to communicate something true about Jesus all the time? Not long ago I wrote a column for Group Magazine titled "Don't Be Safe." I wrote it because I was hearing so many teenagers and adults say goodbye to each other by advising each other to "Be safe!" I made the case that admonishing each other to remember to guard our safety has nothing to do with Christ following. I offered a list of alternate goodbye statements that communicate something more Jesus-centered—here's a little sampler:
  —*Be Christ's!* I remember an old story that J. Sidlow Baxter, the venerable English pastor and author, used to tell about a retired Scottish pastor he often passed on the lane near his home. Baxter once asked the old man, "How are you keeping?" The man responded, "I'm not keeping, I'm kept." Of all the things we can "be," nothing beats "Christ's."[2]
  —*Stay awake!* I think much of our culture is living life asleep at the wheel—that's one reason why we see so many roadside wrecks in families today. Jesus told us to stay alert because there's a "roaring lion" stalking us—he wasn't kidding.
  —*Be strong and courageous!* When God placed the mantle of leadership on Joshua after Moses' death, he charged him to be "strong and courageous" three times in four verses (Joshua 1:6-9).
  —*Be true!* Rather than elevating safety as our filtering lens, how about reminding each other to speak and live the truth in every environment?
  —*Live large!* This one's a favorite of my friend Bob Krulish. Living small means to live disconnected from our true nature and calling—living large means to agree with Jesus about our place in his great rescue operation.
- *Games*—Now, of course, not every game has to be specifically about Jesus—Capture the Flag (With Jesus' Face on It). But if we're "saturating" kids with the beeline, I think it's great to look for the beeline to Jesus in every game we play and then use the game as a discussion starter or as merely an example in a Jesus-centered conversation.

---

2 From a sermon given by J. Sidlow Baxter at Calvary Temple Church in Denver, Colorado, in 1984.

- *Conversations*—So how do we saturate our conversations with beelines to Jesus? I think the key is to listen well when kids tell us stories about their life and then continually ask for more details—trying to find something in the young person's conversation that would link to a Jesus-centered question or bridge. Some standard conversational Jesus-centered questions or bridges include

  "That reminds me so much of when Jesus said/did…"

  "That's a tough one—doesn't it make you wonder what Jesus would've done in your shoes?"

  "This morning/afternoon/evening I was reading in one of the gospels, and Jesus said/did something just like what you're talking about."

  "I've learned something from Jesus about this…"

  "If you'd invited him, do you think Jesus would have gone with you to do that?"

  OK, the first time you do this—like anything—it's pretty clunky. But the more often you practice, the more natural it becomes. Soon, it will be like breathing for you. The goal, remember, is to point back to Jesus in everything you do. Try it out first with your family—play with it until you feel comfortable taking it outside your family and within your youth ministry.

- *Voice-mail messages*—Consider changing your voice-mail message every week to include a very short statement in your message that replicates one of the alternate "goodbyes" I've listed earlier. For example, after your standard "I'm not here" message, simply close by saying "Be Christ's."

- *E-mailing and text messaging*—When I return e-mails, I have a "signature" function that automatically gets added to the end of my messages. If you have the same feature, consider including a Jesus-centered message with your signature. For example: "I have determined to know nothing by Jesus Christ, and him crucified." Or if you're text messaging, consider signing each message with a Jesus-centered "icon" such as "4JC."

- *Meals*—How about surprising your kids with alternative, Jesus-centered ways to say "grace" before your shared meals? Instead of bowing your heads and solemnly repeating your standard thanks for the food before you, what if you, instead, asked everyone to raise a glass to Jesus and then toasted him? Or what if you asked everyone to loudly whisper a cheer—"Jesus!"—all at the same time? Or what if you quoted a Jesus-centered Scripture passage such as: "Now to Him who is able to do far more abundantly beyond all that we ask or think, according to the power that works within us, to Him be the glory in the church and in Christ Jesus to all generations forever and ever. Amen" (Ephesians 3:20-21)?

The point, of course, is to teach ourselves to see the beeline in everything we do, and train others to do the same. That's what I call "saturation."

THE BURNING MAGNIFYING GLASS

When I was a kid I didn't have the following toys, gadgets, or devices:

- video games
- Internet
- iPod
- Walkman
- motorized scooter
- Game Boy
- cell phone
- personal computer
- cable TV

Hard to believe, isn't it? And I'm just in my mid-40s.

The "electronic football" I played when I was a kid involved plugging in a little football field, arranging 11 little plastic men on plastic platforms on offense and defense, and then turning on the switch so the field emitted a good "buzz," thus moving the little plastic men randomly toward each other (or not).

When I was really young, I played mostly with my G.I. Joe army men. But I did have what I considered a cutting-edge toy that gave my G.I. Joe adventures the spark they really needed—it was a magnifying glass.

Let's say my good-guy G.I. Joes were trapped inside a little twig building I'd constructed, and my bad-guy G.I. Joes had thrown some toilet paper inside the building (for some inexplicable reason). Then, shockingly, the bad guys hauled out a magnifying glass and used it to focus the sun's rays on all that toilet paper—pretty soon, whoosh! Those good-guy G.I. Joes came rushing out of the burning building, where they were forced to engage in hand-to-hand combat with the bad guys (who bore a startling resemblance to the good guys).

To me, the magnifying glass had something like magical ability—I had only a bare idea of how it worked. Well, a magnifying glass is curved slightly to form a convex lens—it bends the light rays from an object so that it appears larger. And when it's placed between an object and direct sunlight, it bends all those light rays into a single point, making that point really, really hot.

Jesus-centered youth ministry is a lot like that magnifying glass—when we use Spurgeon's beeline as the "curved lens" for everything we do, and put it between Jesus and our kids, something flames up. In this case, we're not burning toilet paper—we're lighting a fire in our teenagers, our adult leaders, and ourselves. And this particular fire is a "consuming fire"—that means we all end up consumed by and for Jesus.

And that's a nice description of the Christian life in full—following Christ because you're consumed by him, because he's the hub of your wheel, because you're undeniably, unapologetically, aggressively Jesus-centered. We know the *National Study of Youth and Religion* finds that only 10 percent of us have a "hub" relationship with Jesus—so let's make sure you and I, and the young people we're influencing—are part of that 10 percent.

Let's you and I embrace the beeline.

After all, a "devoted faith" is really just the normal Christian life for those who *appreciate* cup holders but are *obsessed* with drivetrains.

group
magazine®

Equipping Youth Leaders for Over 30 Years

1.800.447.1070 . youthministry.com

For more amazing resources

visit us at
www.group.com...

...or call us at
800-747-6060 ext. 1370!

Incredible things will happen™